2/UL/127882

Cambridge Topics in Geography: second series

Editors Alan R. H. Baker, Emmanuel College, Cambridge
Colin Evans, King's College School, Wimbledon

Migration and geographical change

Philip E. Ogden

Queen Mary and Westfield College, University of London

KT-165-402

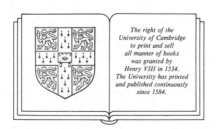

The right of the
University of Cambridge
to print and sell
all manner of books
was granted by
Henry VIII in 1534.
The University has printed
and published continuously
since 1584.

Cambridge University Press

Cambridge
New York   Port Chester
Melbourne   Sydney

Published by the Press Syndicate of the University of Cambridge
The Pitt Building, Trumpington Street, Cambridge CB2 1RP
40 West 20th Street, New York, NY 10011, USA
10 Stamford Road, Oakleigh, Melbourne 3166, Australia

© Cambridge University Press 1984

First published 1984
Fourth printing 1990

Printed in Great Britain at the University Press, Cambridge

Library of Congress catalogue card number: 83–15008

British Library cataloguing in publication data
Ogden, Philip E.
   Migration and geographical change.– (Cambridge
   topics in geography: second series)
   1. Migration, Internal   2. Emigration and
   immigration   3. Population geography
   I. Title
   304.8'09   HB1951

   ISBN 0 521 22686 4 hardback
   ISBN 0 521 22687 2 paperback

We are grateful to the following for permission to reproduce the
photographs;
BBC Hulton Picture Library; p 51 BBC Hulton Picture Library and
The Bettmann Archive; cover and p 1 Camera Press; pp 63, 88 and 99
(Glyn Genin) Fitzwilliam Musuem, Cambridge; p 36 Format
Photographers/Maggie Murray; p 68 Richard and Sally Greenhill; p 72
The John Hillelson Agency; pp 24 (Gilles Peress/Magnum) and 91
(William Karel) Paramount and Kobal Collection; p 75 Rex Features;
pp 34, 41, 47 and 90 Royal Geographical Society; p 13

RD

University Library
– 8 NOV 1990
LANCASTER

To my parents and sister for help and encouragement

DUHV
O
Copy 1

Contents

Preface

Human migration is an attractive subject for the geographer to study. The great diversity of the movements from place to place which have come to characterise human society has had great effects on the geography of the contemporary world. Migration is a phenomenon which concerns individuals: few people now go through life without changing residence several times, thereby influencing and reflecting their employment, education, family and social links. But migration's most obvious effect is on the character of places. The geographer is well placed to evaluate the causes and consequences of migration as well as to describe the patterns of volume, direction and distance which migration flows exhibit.

Migration is part of the wider study of population geography and is one element in the understanding of the geographical organisation of human society. Migration is increasingly a theme of 'A' level geography syllabuses and of course is relevant for those beginning the study of geography in higher education. It is for this audience that the present brief text is intended. The book offers a selective treatment of some key themes in the study of migration, mixing detailed case-studies with more general ideas on ways of analysing and explaining observed patterns and trends. It naturally reflects the author's particular expertise and interests, although an attempt has been made to draw examples from a wide cross-section of cases in different parts of the world.

I am most grateful to the editors of the series and to Ray Hall and Lesley Lee for their comments on the manuscript; to Teresa Anthony for preparing the typescript with such care; and to successive school and undergraduate audiences on whom some of these ideas were first tested.

Philip E. Ogden,
Queen Mary College
University of London, March 1983

1 Introduction

The eyes of departing migrants are fixed on the sea,
Conjuring destinies out of impersonal water:
. . . . .
Red after years of failure or bright with fame,
The eyes of homecomers thank these historical cliffs:
The mirror can no longer lie nor the clock reproach;
In the shadow under the yew at the children's party,
Everything must be explained.

W. H. Auden, *Dover*, August 1937

Migration and geographical change

Human migration is deeply embedded in both the history and present functioning of modern society. At the broadest scale international migrations have played a major role in shaping the world cultural map: immigration is at the very root of societies like the United States, Canada or Australia and has profoundly marked many countries of Latin America or Africa. Europe, once the great exporter of people to these countries, became a net importer of labour in recent decades: there are approximately fifteen million labour migrants in Western European countries at present. The numbers of people involved may indeed be enormous: some 67 million people crossed an ocean between 1800 and 1950, of whom 60 million were Europeans and of these two out of every three went to the USA; some 10 million Italians left home to settle abroad between 1846 and 1932; there are many more people of Irish origin living outside Ireland, in the USA or Britain especially, than within it. Equally, it has been estimated that some 7.7 million people were involved in intra-

Migrants coming to America on board the S.S Westernland. This picture was taken in 1890, a time of great immigration to the United States from many parts of Europe. Over the century 1830–1932 the USA received some 24 million immigrants.

1

European movement associated with World War I, while the Second World War was accompanied by massive shifts of population involving more than 25 million people. An entirely contemporary example is that of the Gulf states: by the late 1970s oil-induced economic growth meant that states like Kuwait or the United Arab Emirates had over 50% migrants in their population. Another is the sudden expulsion of some 2 million illegal migrants, mainly Ghanaians, from Nigeria in 1983.

Yet we should not lose sight of the fact that migration involves individuals: we need look only at the experience of our own families to see the way in which geographical and social mobility work. Many people reading this book will have changed residence in the last few years; most are likely to migrate several times during their lifetime. A simple questionnaire amongst a group of twenty undergraduates at Queen Mary College, London, taking a population geography course in 1983 revealed the extent of their mobility. Only seven were still living in the same town where they were born (excluding the move to university), and of these only three had not changed residence within the town. The number of permanent changes of residence up to the time of going to university averaged three, with one case of thirteen moves (reflecting the father's occupation in the Royal Navy) and another involving residence in Italy, Yugoslavia and South Africa (father a diplomat). Whilst only three students had ever lived outside the UK and only two had parents born outside the country, all but one had travelled extensively in Europe and ten in countries beyond. Amongst parents of the students, sixteen fathers out of twenty and seventeen mothers had moved away from their town or village of birth. This group is scarcely a representative or scientific sample but, bearing in mind that they are nineteen- and twenty-year-olds, it is some indication of the degree of mobility experienced and likely to follow in the remaining fifty or sixty years of their lifetime.

Between these two extreme scales – of mass migrations on the one hand and their individual components on the other – comes a huge range of movements at different scales and with widely differing economic and social causes and consequences. Migration has been studied from a variety of disciplinary viewpoints – economics, sociology and economic history for example – but it is in essence a geographical phenomenon. The general theme of this book, therefore, is the relationship between migration and geographical change. Inevitably, much must be omitted in a brief survey of this kind, but to give an impression of the breadth of interest which migration study has embraced, the text is divided into five sections, in addition to the preliminary remarks of this chapter. A general review of migration theories and methods of analysis in Chapter 2 is followed by three chapters dealing with migration and its effects at progressively finer scales: international movement, the relationship between migration and urban growth and the study of migrants in the city. A last chapter recognises that much movement, particularly at present, is related to political attitudes and governmental control and with case studies of the UK, Australia and the USSR shows how policies work in practice.

There is a deliberate attempt here to focus less on the technical and quantitative aspects of migration study, with which at times geographers have been too much occupied, and more on the broad effects of migration at world, regional and city scales, to hint repeatedly both at the

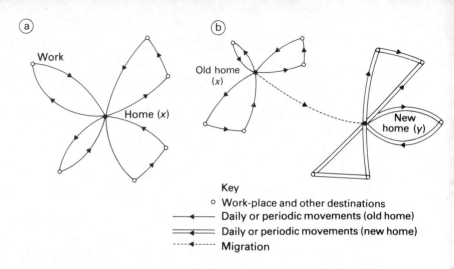

Fig 1.1 A schematic representation of the distinction between (a) circulation and (b) migration. Around a place of residence, an individual may develop complex daily or periodic movements for work, shopping or leisure. The change of residence from *x* to *y* is termed migration and at point *y* a new pattern of circulation arises. *Source:* based on Open University (1974), *Social Sciences, a third level course, unit 9, Human Migration*, p. 9.

Key
○ Work-place and other destinations
———◄——— Daily or periodic movements (old home)
═══◄═══ Daily or periodic movements (new home)
----◄----- Migration

historical dimensions to present patterns of human mobility and at the relevance of migration to contemporary social issues such as migration policy and racial discrimination. The emphasis is upon permanent or semi-permanent migrations, their causes and effects, rather than on temporary or daily patterns of mobility, which are not treated in this volume.

Some simple definitions

Simple definitions are possible, although in practice they are sometimes made more complex by, for example, the variety of movements involved, the scale at which they take place and difficulties over sources for their study. A general distinction is usually made between mobility, which is a very general term covering all kinds of territorial movements, both temporary and permanent over various distances, and migration, which is more restricted in meaning, implying a permanent or semi-permanent change of residence. The latter would thus not include such movements as journey to work, tourism, recreation or shopping excursions which are often grouped under a general heading of circulation, where no change of residence is implied. In its simplest form (Fig. 1.1) we may think of these definitions as applied to the individual who has a permanent place of residence (*x*) from which he may make a number of moves, to work, leisure or on holiday, for example, which do not imply a permanent change of residence. If the latter does take place (to point *y*), then this is a clear form of migration and from this new point the individual establishes a new form of mobility or circulation. From birth to death almost every individual experiences a number of permanent moves in different stages of life in relation, for example, to marriage, job-seeking or retirement.

It is these changes of residence which form the background to themes treated in this text, although the importance of temporary, daily or seasonal mobility and its geographical impact is not underestimated. In addition, some moves fall outside these simple definitions: nomads, for example, move constantly with no permanent residential base; seasonal migration in traditional societies often involved absence for months at a time; and those owning two homes have two separate centres around which a mobility pattern is established. In practice, even defining migration fairly loosely as a permanent or semi-permanent change of residence may create difficulties when applied to particular cases, and

3

some forms of movement may have to be treated as special cases according to the aims of the study and the type of data available.

Further factors may, however, help to refine our simple definitions.

(a) First, a definition based on the origins and destinations of migrants, and used in part in this book: for example, international migrations (from state to state), rural–urban (from countryside to town) or urban–rural, inter-urban (between cities), intra-urban (within cities) or frontierward migrations (towards a new frontier of settlement) are all valid distinctions.

(b) Secondly, moves may further be classified according to distance moved, since there is clearly a great potential difference between a move from one house to another in the same street and a migration between continents. Yet classification by distance is fraught with difficulties: distance is in fact rarely measured directly; rather, migration is recorded when an administrative boundary is crossed. Thus, moves within administrative units may never be recorded at all. Equally, although most studies including the present one adopt the distinction between 'internal' moves, within a country, and international flows, we should be aware that this may be rather artificial: a migrant within a large country such as India or China may move a much longer distance and be subject to much greater social and cultural change than, say, the migrant who simply crosses the border between two neighbouring European states, for example Austria and Germany. Finally, we should in any case beware of attaching too great a significance to geographical distance, whose precise influence may be tempered by the associated changes in the migrant's lifestyle and cultural surroundings.

(c) A third definitional tool, as hinted above, is time: migrations may vary from permanent moves, from which the migrant never returns, to short-term seasonal labour migrations. Since permanent changes of residence often succeed one another throughout the life cycle it is of interest to analyse the determinants of the timing of such moves. One form of migration may lead to others; for example, seasonal migration of workers in nineteenth-century France certainly led in some cases to permanent migrations, although recent research has shown that some at least of these migrants eventually returned home at the end of their working lives. Return migrations are indeed of considerable contemporary interest: from Western Europe, for example, migrant workers returning home to Italy, Greece, Turkey and so on, as the economic climate changes; or retirement migrations within countries such as France or Italy from town to countryside.

(d) A fourth means of classification is based on the motivations and causes underlying migration. A key distinction is between forced and free movement. Major examples of the former include slavery, refugee movement or other migrations which result from political pressures. Although some would argue that the degree of 'freedom' involved is only relative, we generally group into the second category migrations for economic or social causes, for example labour, retirement or educational migration.

In summary, therefore, recent attempts to provide a classification of migrations recognise that the following need to be taken into account: distance (long, short); time (temporary, permanent); boundaries crossed (internal, international); areas involved (between, or within, cities or rural areas); decision-making and political influence (forced or free); other causes (economic or non-economic); numbers involved (individual or mass migrations) and the social organisation and characteristics of migrants (family, class or individual). It is this very complexity of possible types as we shall see in the following chapter, that has done much to make the search for a comprehensive theory of migration more difficult.

The simple description of migration also requires us to be careful in the use of terms. Where migration takes place within a country we usually refer to in-migration and out-migration, while for external migrations we refer to immigration and emigration. A group of migrants with a common origin and destination we refer to as a migration stream, while the term gross migration refers to the total number of in-migrants and out-migrants and is sometimes referred to as the turnover for a given area. The difference between the two streams would be net migration or the migration balance. In describing the way migration takes place, two frequently encountered terms are step migration, where the migration system from countryside to large city may be seen as composed of a series of steps or stages of movement (for example countryside to small town, small town to large city or large city to metropolis). Chain migration, on the other hand, implies that an initial migration stream of innovators who make the first moves from home are followed by a secondary group. For example, a primary group may be dominated by younger adult males in search of better employment or a better standard of living while the secondary group may be their dependants, wives, children or parents, as well as neighbours and other members of the home community. Colonisation comes into this category—where a group of pioneer migrants is followed by a growing stream of colonists. Chain migration makes itself felt in the contemporary city too, where the concentration of an immigrant group may be brought about by the initial, sometimes arbitrary, location of the first arrivals who pass on information to subsequent movers.

A most important consideration too is the selectivity of migration. In answering the question, 'Who migrates?', we see that migrants are selected according to a number of characteristics. These include age, where there is a clear tendency for young adults to predominate in migrant flows; education, where those who have spent a longer time in education are most likely to move; sex, where either males or females may in certain economic circumstances be more migratory; and occupation and social status, where a particular job, for example in the professions, may involve greater movement. These influences, some of which are pursued in the next chapter, determine who are the movers and who are the stayers.

Migration and population growth

The extent to which migration contributes to population growth, at any scale of geographical unit, may be simply expressed by the following equation:

$$PC = B - D \pm NM$$

where population change (PC) between two dates is a function of the number of births (B), the number of deaths (D) and net migration (NM). Although, because of difficulties over sources, which rarely allow us to measure every migration, we frequently have to rely on net migration, it is most important to remember that this is simply a balance of inward and outward movement which may mask to a considerable extent the volume of gross migration. In the UK in 1979, for instance, a net migration gain from other countries of 6,000 people concealed an inward flow of some 195,000 and an emigration of some 189,000. A simple example (Table 1.1) at a different scale also shows how important this may be. The author's analysis of 52 small rural parishes in southern France illustrates that an overall population loss of just over one thousand between 1962 and 1968 in fact conceals, if we take as far as possible the actual number of births, deaths, in-migrants and out-migrants, an identifiable total of over 9,000 individuals. This area, which was one of rural decline, was losing population both by out-migration and by an excess of deaths over births.

Table 1.1 Elements of population change in some southern French rural parishes, 1962–68. *Source:* calculated from French censuses and civil registers.

Total change	Natural change			Net migration		
	Births	Deaths	Total	In-	Out-	Total
− 1,025	1,482	1,822	− 340	2,552	3,237	− 685

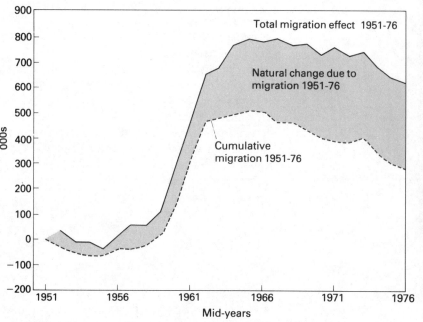

Fig 1.2 The estimated cumulative effect of migration on the population of England and Wales 1951–76. Two elements combine to produce the overall effect: the rate of migration itself and the consequent effect on rates of natural increase (births minus deaths), the latter shown by the shaded area on the graph. Rapid immigration during the late 1950s and very early 1960s produced a very apparent long-term effect, which has been reduced by net outflows of migrants since the mid-1960s. *Source:* adapted from C. Walker and M. Gee (1977) 'Migration: the impact on the population', *Population Trends*, 9:25.

If we take just the net migration figure of − 685, this conceals a gross figure of nearly 6,000 migrants. Net figures are nearly always easier to obtain—we can, for example, calculate net migration for an area simply by knowing the numbers of births and deaths and the total population at the beginning and end of the period studied—and are certainly useful as a starting-point of analysis. Yet we must bear in mind, if we wish to look at the individual decisions migrants take or the effects of migration on origin or destination, that net figures represent no more than a balance.

Migration may be a key factor in population growth both at national and regional scales. Countries like Britain, France and West Germany have experienced considerable immigration in post-war years, which adds both the migrants themselves and eventually the children they bear. Fig. 1.2 shows the estimated cumulative effect of migration to England and Wales

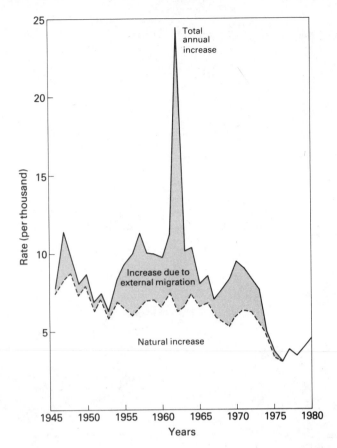

Fig 1.3 Components of population growth in France 1945–80. Emphasises the highly variable nature of the contribution of immigration from abroad. As well as the peak in the early 1960s caused by the repatriation of French citizens from North Africa, note the very considerable contribution of immigration in every year from the mid-1950s to 1974, and its sudden curtailment thereafter. *Source:* G. Calot (1981), The demographic situation in France, *Population Trends*, 25:16.

over the period 1951–76 and its effect on natural change. Fig. 1.3 shows, for France, the highly variable contribution migrants may make: the peak in the early 1960s being the result of massive repatriation of French citizens from their North African colonies to the mainland. Other countries of long-standing immigration, like the USA or Australia, grew for many years as much by immigration as by an excess of births over deaths. Immigration may make a particular contribution to those developed states where the excess of births over deaths is small: between 1950 and 1970, for example, immigration contributed 21% of the total population increase in Belgium, 35% in France, 30% in Sweden, 44% in Switzerland and 45% in West Germany. By contrast, we should add, though, that migration does not invariably contribute significantly to a country's population growth. In the USSR, where external migration is restricted, it is estimated that net emigration in the whole of the post-war period probably amounts to somewhat less than 400,000, or only 0.15% of the 262 million citizens counted in 1979. While emigration is clearly important to the groups concerned—mainly Jews, Germans and Armenians—it has little impact on overall population trends.

Nevertheless in many countries, migrants have a distorting effect on the age and sex structure of the population, for example when a migrant stream consists predominantly of young men or young couples. In England and Wales, those born outside are mainly in the 20–50 age range and this is eventually reflected in an increase in births to this section of the population. By 1980, some 13% of all live births in England and Wales were to mothers born overseas. In Greater London in 1980, 22% of all births were to women whose own birthplace was in the New

Table 1.2 Population growth in England and Wales, 1971–81, for different types of district. *Source:* OPCS Population Statistics Division (1982), 'Recent population growth and the effect of the decline in births', *Population Trends* 27: Tables 1 and 3.

Selected districts	Population 1981 (millions)	Growth 1971–81 (%)	Net migration (%)	Natural change (%)
Inner London boroughs	2.5	− 17.7	− 18.4	+ 0.8
Outer London boroughs	4.2	− 5.0	− 6.4	+ 1.4
Large cities (over 175,000 in 1971)	2.8	− 5.1	− 5.9	+ 0.8
New Town districts	2.2	+ 15.1	+ 9.7	+ 5.4
Resort and seaside retirement districts	3.3	+ 4.9	+ 11.1	− 6.3
Industrial districts in Midlands, E. Anglia and South	3.3	+ 5.0	+ 1.6	+ 3.4
England and Wales	49.0	+ 0.5	− 0.6	+ 1.1

Fig 1.4 Greater London, net migration 1971–81. Total population change in each borough is the product of natural increase and net migration. All boroughs experienced net out-migration, particularly

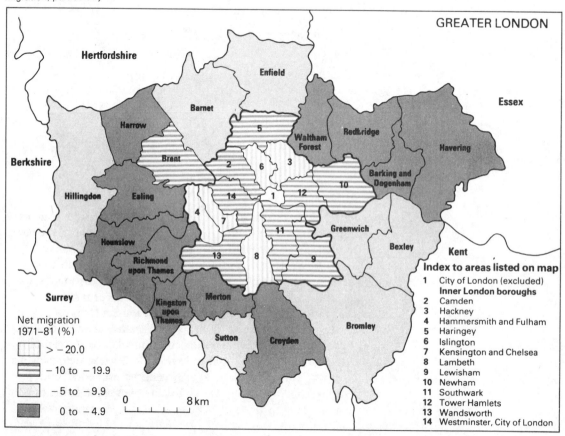

Net migration 1971–81 (%)

- > − 20.0
- − 10 to − 19.9
- − 5 to − 9.9
- 0 to − 4.9

0   8 km

Index to areas listed on map

1 City of London (excluded)
Inner London boroughs
2 Camden
3 Hackney
4 Hammersmith and Fulham
5 Haringey
6 Islington
7 Kensington and Chelsea
8 Lambeth
9 Lewisham
10 Newham
11 Southwark
12 Tower Hamlets
13 Wandsworth
14 Westminster, City of London

marked in Inner London, with losses of over 20% in e.g. Hackney, Islington, Lambeth, and Kensington and Chelsea. Most boroughs experienced small excesses of births over deaths, although some inner boroughs like Tower Hamlets and Southwark lost population through this mechanism also. *Source of data:* OPCS (1982), *Census 1981, County Report, Greater London* (CEN 81 CR 17) p. 3 (HMSO, London).

Commonwealth or Pakistan. Yet migration may also lead to rapid adjustment within the group itself, the level of births and deaths often adapting quite quickly to those of the host society.

Within a country, migration is a major means of population redistribution. Table 1.2 shows for selected districts in England and Wales between 1971 and 1981 that variations in rates of migration are rather greater than in rates of natural change. Out-migration has been the major contributor to the population decline that has marked the evolution of London and other major cities over the decade and this is shown for inner and outer London boroughs in Fig. 1.4. In-migration has added considerably to population growth in New Towns and retirement districts.

Fig 1.5 The effect of areal size, shape and population distribution on the classification of mobility. Moves are recorded as migration when an official boundary used for data collection is crossed (solid line). Moves which do not cross a boundary (broken line) may go unrecorded, although they may cover equal or longer distances. *Source:* based on Jones (1981), p. 203.

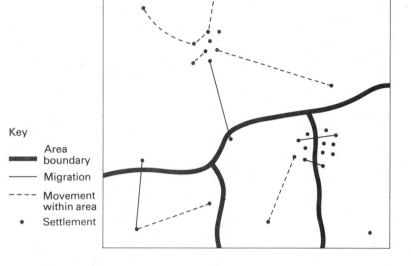

Key

━━━ Area boundary

─── Migration

- - - Movement within area

• Settlement

In the latter, migration compensates for the excess of deaths over births. For England and Wales as a whole, we see that there has been a very low rate of population increase, partly because of a small excess of births over deaths and partly because there were in fact over the last decade more emigrants than immigrants.

Sources

How do we measure migration? Which moves are recorded? Do we know in detail the characteristics of migrants? Do we know what happened in the past as well as in the present? The answers to these questions are varied, but perhaps the most relevant general observation is that a large proportion of moves go entirely unrecorded and even in the most advanced contemporary societies, there is only limited recording of migrants and their characteristics. The nature of sources strongly influences the nature of research. Amongst problems encountered are that, since usually an administrative boundary must be crossed for a move to be recorded, much depends on the nature of the boundaries and areas concerned (an example of the distorting effect of boundaries is given in Fig. 1.5); that recording is sporadic both in the recording of moves and of the characteristics of migrants; and that much information on migration is recorded coincidentally by other surveys (on education or health, for example), whose results may not be generally available to the researcher. Pessimism, however, should not be exaggerated: the volume of studies on migration and their variety shows that problems of sources can be overcome to some extent.

There are three principal sources: the census, the population register and the social survey.

The population census is widely used as a source because it is taken at fairly regular intervals and covers the whole country. It generally provides two sorts of data: birthplaces of the population and period migration figures – that is, movement over a particular period of time. Birthplace tables show the present residence of members of a population against their places of birth. For a national population these would be by other

Table 1.3 Birthplaces of the population of Inner London and of two English towns in 1981. *Source:* Census 1981 County Reports, West Yorkshire Pt I and Tyne and Wear Pt I, Greater London Pt I, Table 10 (OPCS, 1982).

	Bradford		Newcastle upon Tyne		Inner London	
	(no.)	(%)	(no.)	(%)	(no.)	(%)
All residents	454,198	100	272,914	100	2,425,630	100
Birthplaces						
England	399,838	88.03	255,808	93.73	1,741,290	71.79
Scotland	5,522	1.19	5.672	2.01	47,644	1.96
Wales	1,868	0.40	873	0.31	27,617	1.14
Rest of UK	1,977	0.43	951	0.34	18,860	0.78
Irish Republic	3,716	0.80	1,093	0.39	96,728	3.99
Old Commonwealth*	750	0.16	411	0.15	19,140	0.79
New Commonwealth**	12,784	2.76	3,547	1.26	284,874	11.74
Pakistan	17,668	3.81	1,092	0.39	12,964	0.53
Remainder	10,075	2.17	3,467	1.23	176,513	7.28

* Principally Australia, New Zealand, Canada.
**Principally India, Bangladesh, the Caribbean and E. Africa.

countries of birth; for regional populations either by country of birth or by a variety of smaller administrative divisions. For example, the 1981 census for the United Kingdom showed that 18% of the population of Greater London was born outside the UK, a figure which varied between nearly 38% in Kensington and Chelsea and 4% for the outer London borough of Havering. For the metropolitan counties outside London, figures varied between nearly 10% for the West Midlands and under 2% for Tyne and Wear. Table 1.3 gives a detailed breakdown of birthplaces for three rather different cases.

Birthplace data have the advantage of being relatively easy to collect and may give an overall impression of the impact of migration on a community over a long period, but they have disadvantages too. For example, they say nothing about the number of residential moves that may have occurred between birth and present residence nor about the length of stay at origin or destination, and they cover a time-period which is as variable as the ages of the population. Equally, they take no account of the fact that many people born outside the area of census may have moved with their parents rather than independently. Thus, a sixty-year-old man living in London at the time of the 1981 census may have been born in Glasgow, but may have moved from there to Manchester with his parents—keeping no recollection of Scotland or even a Scottish accent—and then may have arrived in London via a series of other moves related to his work or family, the subtleties of which are lost in the birthplace tabulations. Similarly, his next-door neighbour living in London in 1981 may have been born there but may have spent a good deal of his life elsewhere. Nevertheless, it was sources such as these from the census of England and Wales which Ravenstein used in his work a hundred years ago on the 'laws of migration' (see Chapter 2) and which have been used a great deal subsequently.

A second form of data from the census relies on questions being asked about the place of residence at some previous date, for example the time of the previous census or perhaps one, five or ten years previously. Again, much depends on the administrative boundaries taken and, over a ten-year period, for example, many moves may still go unrecorded. Yet at its best this may be a valuable source of information especially when, as is the case in many developed countries, an attempt is made to collect related data on migrants' economic and social characteristics. Direct collection of data on migration is relatively recent: from 1940 in the USA

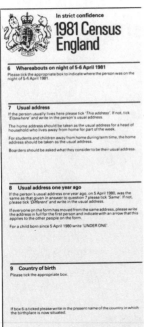

In strict confidence

1981 Census England

6 **Whereabouts on night of 5-6 April 1981**
Please tick the appropriate box to indicate where the person was on the night of 5-6 April 1981.

7 **Usual address**
If the person usually lives here please tick 'This address'. If not, tick 'Elsewhere' and write in the person's usual address.

The home address should be taken as the usual address for a head of household who lives away from home for part of the week.

For students and children away from home during term time, the home address should be taken as the usual address.

Boarders should be asked what they consider to be their usual address.

8 **Usual address one year ago**
If the person's usual address one year ago, on 5 April 1980, was the same as that given in answer to question 7 please tick 'Same'. If not, please tick 'Different' and write in the person's usual address.

If everyone on the form has moved from the same address, please write the address in full for the first person and indicate with an arrow that this applies to the other people on the form.

For a child born since 5 April 1980 write 'UNDER ONE'.

9 **Country of birth**
Please tick the appropriate box.

If box 6 is ticked please write in the present name of the country in which the birthplace is now situated.

The 1981 census for England is a major source of information on population migration. For example, question 8 provides data on changes of residence over the previous year and question 9 on place of birth. This information is thus available for the whole of the population and may be correlated with question 7 and with other data on individuals and households gathered by the census.

and 1961 in the British census. The 1981 British census asked for birthplace (question 9) and place of residence a year before (question 8). When these are compared with usual address (question 7) we can begin to trace migration patterns, while other information on occupation, age and sex allow us to establish migrants' characteristics. These data are usually presented in summary form by the census office.

A further type of information comes from the census enumerators' manuscript returns which give a person-by-person listing of inhabitants, along with a variety of information concerning sex, age, occupation and birthplace. Often the demands of confidentiality mean that these are not made available to the researcher until a long period—in Britain, a century—has elapsed. Thus, important recent work in Britain has been carried out for the mid-nineteenth century. This allows us to analyse not only origins by birthplace but also, aided by such sources as city directories, rate-books, and even personal diaries, to trace the movement of people between successive censuses.

The population register provides a still richer potential source, since it aims to record every move, rather than simply those caught by the rather arbitrary administrative and period framework of the census. Japan, the Netherlands, Belgium, West Germany and most Eastern European states have registers, but perhaps the Scandinavian countries provide the best examples. Recording demographic events such as migration is the primary purpose of such registers rather than simply the by-product of other administrative needs. A recent study in Norway, for example, was able to take all men aged sixteen to sixty-seven in 1971 resident in Norway over the years 1965–1971 and to show the month, year, regional origin and regional destination of each move, as well as the age, marital status, income, wealth and employment of the mover in 1970. In some cases, indeed, if no aggregation of the information is officially made, the researcher may be faced with an overwhelming body of information. In Britain, no population registers of this kind exist except for a brief and rather unrepresentative period immediately after the Second World War.

In Britain, as in many countries, however, there are partial registers which record movements for some parts of the population—for example, electoral lists, files of public utilities like electricity or gas, tax registers, local authority housing registers, school rolls, employee records and so on. A rich source in Britain would be the records of the National Health Service, for example, which note change of doctor and thereby change of residence. There is much potential too in the increasingly computerised and centralised recording of information about individuals, including their mobility, but questions of confidentiality and abuse of such information are frequently raised. This is particularly so in the sensitive matter of ethnicity: in Britain, for example, a proposal to include a question on race or ethnic origin in the 1981 census was dropped after opposition from various groups.

The third main source relates to specific surveys used to supplement available forms of data. An example from Britain is the International Passenger Survey, a sample survey carried out at seaports and airports by the Social Survey Division of the Office of Population Censuses and Surveys. It was set up to give information on tourism and the effect of travel expenditure on the balance of payments, but it also gives figures on international migration. An example of the data collected for the UK is

Fig 1.6 International migration to and from the UK, 1979. Based on data from the International Passenger Survey which interviews samples of passengers at air and sea ports. 29% of those arriving in 1979 (a) came from Pakistan and Commonwealth countries in the Caribbean, Africa and India, a similar proportion to 1969. Only 27% of those leaving (b) went to Australia, Canada and New Zealand compared with 48% in 1969. *Source:* OPCS (1981) *Spotlight* 4, International Migration (HMSO, London).

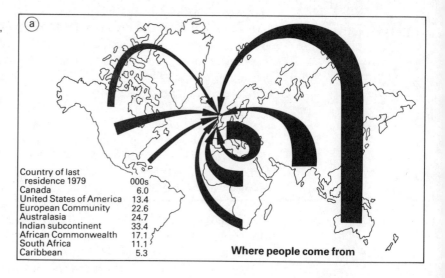

Country of last residence 1979	000s
Canada	6.0
United States of America	13.4
European Community	22.6
Australasia	24.7
Indian subcontinent	33.4
African Commonwealth	17.1
South Africa	11.1
Caribbean	5.3

Where people come from

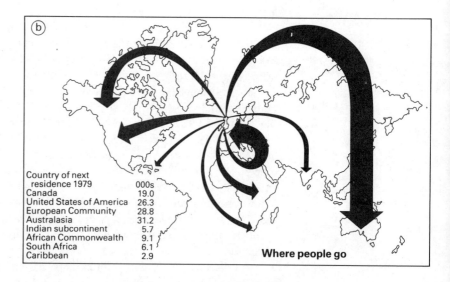

Country of next residence 1979	000s
Canada	19.0
United States of America	26.3
European Community	28.8
Australasia	31.2
Indian subcontinent	5.7
African Commonwealth	9.1
South Africa	6.1
Caribbean	2.9

Where people go

shown in Fig. 1.6. In the USA a Current Population Survey, conducted each month by the Bureau of Census, records changes in residence, supplementing for example the annual Housing Survey. In Britain, the annual General Household Survey of 15,000 households provides similar data, which may be supplemented by information from the biennial (from 1979) Labour Force Survey. Added to these are a large number of surveys of smaller samples, often conducted by individual researchers to answer their detailed questions. An example of a specific source of data on international migrations for European countries is the 'system for the permanent recording of migrations' run by the Organisation for Economic Cooperation and Development, based in Paris.

For the present, as for the past, then, the researcher relies on piecing together the complexity of mobility of individuals and communities from a variety of often diverse and sometimes rather ingeniously exploited sources.

2 Ways of analysing migration

Introduction

Geographers and others working in the field of migration have made various attempts to develop models and theories in an effort to make sense both of the geographical pattern of migration and of underlying explanations for that pattern. Beginning with the great diversity of possible types of movement in space and time which we outlined in Chapter 1, the sorts of questions geographers go on to ask are: 'Is there a geographical pattern to movement?' 'Do laws and theories govern movement?' 'What are the characteristics of migrants?' 'What are the causes and consequences of individual moves?'

This chapter outlines a number of different approaches to these questions.

First, there is the very generalised model of the so-called mobility transition which seeks to provide a framework to explain the relationship between economic and social changes—the process of modernisation—and different forms of mobility.

Secondly, simple laws and models of migration have been developed to describe migration trends. These include attempts by Ravenstein and others to define migration 'laws', as well as the idea of the gravity model and more complex statistical models based upon it. We pay particular attention to the latter in the third section, as well as to the relationship between movement and distance.

Fourthly, we introduce the notion of a systems approach to the study of migration. This in turn leads to separate consideration of the influence

E.G. Ravenstein (1834–1913) was one of the first scholars to suggest that clear 'laws of migration' characterised migrants, their origins and destinations and the nature of migration streams. He developed these ideas in three papers published in 1876, 1885 and 1889.

of economic factors, particularly 'push' and 'pull' influences on migration; social and political factors which may be both cause and result of migration; and lastly we review a group of ideas which see the behaviour of the individual as one key to a migrant's decision to move: his view of the world, his access to information and his ability to make use of it. This approach through the individual is often in sharp distinction to those economic theories, for example, which seek very general relationships in the economy as a whole.

It should be stressed at the outset, however, that despite this daunting body of material, there is still no one, comprehensive, theory of migration and that much work remains to be done in describing and explaining the features of migration flows, their causes and impact.

A broad view: the idea of the 'mobility transition'

One way of setting the rather bewildering variety of population migrations, and their evolution over time, in context has been provided by the American geographer Wilbur Zelinsky. He proposes the idea of the 'mobility transition' by which he implies that 'there are definite patterned regularities in the growth of personal mobility through space-time during recent history, and these regularities comprise an essential component of the modernisation process'. He borrows the term 'transition' from the more widely known term 'demographic transition', a general model which describes the long-term evolution of birth and death rates, and says that just as the latter have declined as societies modernise, so are there parallels in the evolution of human mobility. Five stages of change are recognised in the mobility transition from the pre-modern traditional society (phase I), through the early and late transitional societies (phases II and III) to the advanced and super-advanced societies (phases IV and V). He then further divides mobility into distinct categories: international, frontierward, rural–urban, urban–urban, intra-urban and circulation. This last term implies a whole variety of movements not included under the general heading of migration (see the distinction drawn in Chapter 1). They are usually short-term, repetitive movements: for example, weekend or seasonal movements by students, holidays, shopping trips, hospital and church visits, journey to work, social visits and so on. Several of these categories are treated separately in subsequent chapters of this book. Fig. 2.1 shows the main characteristics of each phase in both the demographic transition (or 'vital' transition, as Zelinsky terms it) and changes in personal mobility. Then in graphical form it shows the way in which each type of population movement is said to react to increasing 'modernisation'.

The general transition is from severely limited geographical and social mobility towards much wider and more elaborate forms of movement, and there are orderly changes in both the intensity of movement and its form—duration, periodicity, distance, categories of migrants, classes of origin and destination and, we might add, geographical impact. Thus, in phase I there is little genuine residential migration and a limited amount of circulation occasioned by social visits, the local economy (commerce and markets for example), war and religion. In phase II, large-scale movements begin to take place: for example, movement from the countryside to the city, movements of emigrants to new lands, pushing

The vital transition	The mobility transition	

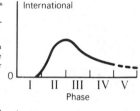

International

Phase A: *The pre-modern traditional society*
(1) A moderately high to quite high fertility pattern that tends to fluctuate only slightly
(2) Mortality at nearly the same level as fertility on the average, but fluctuating much more from year to year
(3) Little, if any, long-range natural increase or decrease

Phase I: *The pre-modern traditional society*
(1) Little genuine residential migration and only such limited circulation as is sanctioned by customary practice in land utilisation, social visits, commerce, warfare, or religious observances

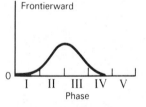

Frontierward

Phase B: *The early transitional society*
(1) Slight, but significant, rise in fertility, which then remains fairly constant at a high level
(2) Rapid decline in mortality
(3) A relatively rapid rate of natural increase, and thus a major growth in size of population

Phase II: *The early transitional society*
(1) Massive movement from countryside to cities, old and new
(2) Significant movement of rural folk to colonisation frontiers, if land suitable for pioneering is available within country
(3) Major outflows of emigrants to available and attractive foreign destinations
(4) Under certain circumstances, a small, but significant, immigration of skilled workers, technicians, and professionals from more advanced parts of the world
(5) Significant growth in various kinds of circulation

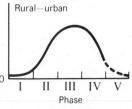

Rural—urban

Phase C: *The late transitional society*
(1) A major decline in fertility, initially rather slight and slow, later quite rapid, until another slowdown occurs as fertility approaches mortality level
(2) A continuing, but slackening, decline in mortality
(3) A significant, but decelerating, natural increase, at rates well below those observed during Phase B

Phase III: *The late transitional society*
(1) Slackening, but still major, movement from countryside to city
(2) Lessening flow of migrants to colonisation frontiers
(3) Emigration on the decline or may have ceased altogether
(4) Further increases in circulation, with growth in structural complexity

Phase D: *The advanced society*
(1) The decline in fertility has terminated, and a socially controlled fertility oscillates rather unpredictably at low to moderate levels
(2) Mortality is stabilised at levels near or slightly below fertility with little year-to-year variability
(3) There is either a light to moderate rate of natural increase or none at all

Phase IV: *The advanced society*
(1) Residential mobility has levelled off and oscillates at a high level
(2) Movement from countryside to city continues but is further reduced in absolute and relative terms
(3) Vigorous movement of migrants from city to city and within individual urban agglomerations
(4) If a settlement frontier has persisted, it is now stagnant or actually retreating
(5) Significant net immigration of unskilled and semi-skilled workers from relatively underdeveloped lands
(6) There may be a significant international migration or circulation of skilled and professional persons, but direction and volume of flow depend on specific conditions
(7) Vigorous accelerating circulation, particularly the economic and pleasure-orientated, but other varieties as well

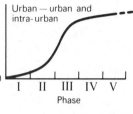

Urban — urban and intra-urban

Phase E: *A future super-advanced society*
(1) No plausible predictions of fertility behaviour are available, but it is likely that births will be more carefully controlled by individuals – and perhaps by new socio-political means
(2) A stable mortality pattern slightly below present levels seems likely, unless organic diseases are controlled and lifespan is greatly extended

Phase V: *A future super-advanced society*
(1) There may be a decline in level of residential migration and a deceleration in some forms of circulation as better communication and delivery systems are instituted
(2) Nearly all residential migration may be of the inter-urban and intraurban variety
(3) Some further immigration of relatively unskilled labour from less developed areas is possible
(4) Further acceleration in some current forms of circulation and perhaps the inception of new forms
(5) Strict political control of internal as well as international movements may be imposed

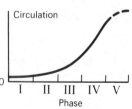

Circulation

(*a*) The phases of the mobility transition and their relationship to the phases of the vital transition

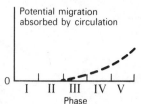

Potential migration absorbed by circulation

Fig 2.1 Zelinsky's hypothesis of the mobility transition. The intensity of different types of migration (international, rural-urban etc.) is related to stages of social development from the pre-modern traditional society to the so-called future super-advanced society. *Source:* adapted from W. Zelinsky (1971), 'The hypothesis of the mobility transition,' *Geographical Review* 61:219–49.

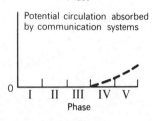

Potential circulation absorbed by communication systems

(*b*) Changes in the volume of different kinds of mobility during the five phases of the mobility transition

back frontiers of settlement through colonisation. Two classic examples of this phase are treated later in this book: emigration to the USA (Chapter 3) and urbanisation in Britain (Chapter 4). These are aspects of the mobility transition most associated with agricultural and industrial revolution and with the spread of towns. In many senses the features of this 'phase' are the most marked and the most widespread in their effects: Zelinsky contends that only a few remote, primitive communities remain untouched. He shows how from the 'point of ignition in England' the impulse to move 'outward or cityward' engulfed Europe and by the mid-twentieth century most other parts of the world. Different states thus pass through his 'phases' at different dates, and he emphasises that many underdeveloped countries are still in phase II, where the modernisation process is both incomplete and dangerously unbalanced.

In phase III, the model sketches changes which have occurred in some countries and are yet to do so in others. The general trend is for a slackening, although still very important, move from countryside to towns, a lessening in emigration and a further increase in both the volume and complexity of circulation. In phase IV, the 'advanced' society, new forms of movement begin to dominate: with the progress of urbanisation, movement of migrants between cities and within cities becomes important. With improvements in living standards and transport—the further widespread diffusion of the motor-car for example—circulation continues to grow apace, while there may be new migrations of unskilled workers from less developed countries and some international movement of skilled and professional people. These features may be found in modern Britain: rural–urban movement has indeed played itself out, to be replaced by movement between and within the great cities, circulation of all sorts has increased, mass emigration at least on the scale of last century has ceased and has been supplanted by the 'brain drain' and by immigration of unskilled labour from, for example, the Caribbean, India and Pakistan. For the United States, similar trends are noted. Circulation is difficult to assess, but Zelinsky notes the increase of motor-vehicle passenger travel in the USA from 252,257 million vehicle-miles in 1940 to 783,687 million in 1967. International tourism is a further example: the total number of international tourists reported to the United Nations Statistical Office rose from 14 million in 1948 to nearly 170 million twenty years later.

In phase V, the model speculates upon the likely trends in mobility in a so-called super-advanced society, where technological progress has much effect on aspects of everyday life. For example, almost all permanent migration is confined to moves between or within cities, and some forms of circulation may increase and so perhaps remove the need for permanent changes of residence. There may be some decline too in circulation as the spread of better communications (via microchip technology, perhaps) make it less necessary for people actually to move from place to place. No region falls fully into this category yet, but those most likely to approach it are Southern California and highly urbanised Japan or other parts of the USA. The graphs in Fig. 2.1 further show how the types of mobility vary with each of the phases of transition. So international and rural–urban movements peak sharply and go into decline, while urban movements and circulation patterns rise quickly. It is an interesting exercise to try to fit individual countries and migration types into this model, which provides a broad descriptive framework. Yet, along with many ambitious models, it has obvious drawbacks. Like its sister model of the 'vital' transition of birth and death rates, the mobility model has great drawbacks for predicting the likely experiences of presently underdeveloped states. Equally, it pays too little attention to the factors explaining changing mobility and how these may be affected by cultural differences, and to the characteristics and behavioural patterns of the migrants, which may be socially much more important than the superficial changes in mobility types. Nevertheless, the model provides a useful starting-point and a framework into which some of the material in this book may be placed.

Some simple laws: Ravenstein and Lee

The idea of the mobility transition owes much to the often-quoted attempt to devise detailed 'laws' of migration by Ravenstein. His ideas, although dating from the 1880s, still retain much validity and, in some respects at least, have been little improved upon. He based his work on birthplace data for Britain in 1871 and 1881, and later included material from similar sources for North America and Europe. His problem was to discover whether, from the great mass of movements recorded in the data, he could distinguish any organising principles. At its simplest, migration reflects factors associated with area of origin and destination and characteristics of the migration stream and the migrants themselves. Ravenstein's laws may be stated as follows:

(1) The majority of migrants go only a short distance.
(2) Migration proceeds step by step.
(3) Migrants going long distances generally go by preference to one of the great centres of commerce or industry.
(4) Each current of migration produces a compensating counter-current.
(5) The natives of towns are less migratory than those of rural areas.
(6) Females are more migratory than males within the kingdom of their birth, but males more frequently venture beyond.
(7) Most migrants are adults; families rarely migrate out of their country of birth.
(8) Large towns grow more by migration than by natural increase.
(9) Migration increases in volume as industries and commerce develop and transport improves.
(10) The major direction of migration is from the agricultural areas to the centres of industry and commerce.
(11) The major causes of migration are economic.

We can thus see that it is the simple points made in (9) and (10) that underlie the ideas of mobility transition and there is no doubt that . Ravenstein in general identified questions of continuing relevance. His ideas have been variously taken up and refined, using much more varied data and regional cases than he was able to do and, given that he was working largely in the England of a century ago, it is remarkable that his ideas have endured. There is certainly an inverse relationship between migration and distance; the idea of there being currents and counter-currents seems valid; as does the link between economic development and migration. That migration proceeds step by step may be true in some

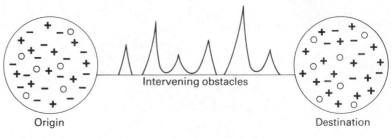

Fig 2.2 Lee's idea of the variety of influences on migration. Each place of origin and destination has numerous attracting, repelling and neutral factors, while between origin and destination a number of intervening obstacles exist. The latter include, for example, distance, means of transport and legal restraints. *Source:* E. Lee (1966), 'A theory of migration', *Demography* 3:48.

Origin

Destination

+ Attracting factors
− Repelling factors
○ Neutral factors

cases, though not inevitably so and current knowledge of the nineteenth century as well as subsequent experience of the twentieth throws doubt on the extent to which females are more migratory than males, on the propensity of families to move and on the role of natural increase and migration in stimulating urban growth. In the developed world, as we have seen, the rural−urban movements which Ravenstein observed have now been replaced by urban−rural movements or those between cities and his statement that the major causes of migration are economic needs to be qualified with reference both to social and political factors and to the scale of the movement in question.

Several authors have further refined Ravenstein's ideas, of whom perhaps the best known is Lee. He suggests (see Fig. 2.2) that we can isolate four classes of factors which underlie the decision to migrate: those associated with the place of origin; those associated with the place of destination; intervening obstacles that lie between the places of origin and destination; and a variety of personal factors which moderate these influences. The characteristics of origin and destination may be seen as having positive effects (+ in the diagram), encouraging movement; negative effects (−), discouraging movement; and neutral factors (0) to which people are indifferent. The operation of these factors depends on the individual: what is attractive to one person is not necessarily so to another. There is also a difference in the operation of the factors at origin and destination: the latter is always less well-known and, as Lee says, there remains an 'element of ignorance or even mystery' about it. This would be clearly so in the case of international migrations (see Chapter 3) where much 'knowledge' is based on hearsay and speculation. In addition, between origin and destination, a number of intervening obstacles exist: these include distance itself but also the means of transport and more definite restraints like immigration laws, quotas by national origin of migrants, or physical restraints like the Berlin Wall.

Lee uses the above ideas to formulate a series of hypotheses relating to the volume of movement; the tendency for streams and counterstreams of migrants to develop; and the characteristics of migrants, particularly that migrants are not random samples of the population at origin but are selected by reason of their educational, health or economic status. Other authors have further refined these ideas: the keener reader may wish to take up the ideas of Todaro, for example, who has been working with evidence from developing countries.

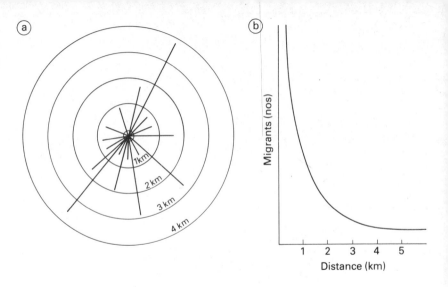

Fig 2.3 Simple aspects of migration and distance. Equidistant bands may be drawn around the destination of migrants and straight-line distances measured (a). These may then be graphed to reveal the relationship between distance and the volume of migration. This pattern could represent, for example, a small market town attracting migrants from neighbouring villages.

Simple spatial models

One example of the ideas taken up and developed with greatest success by geographers is those dealing with the influence of distance. Does distance have an effect on migration? Does that effect vary with the type of migration and factors such as the social class, age and sex of migrants? Does the influence of distance vary over time? For many migrations it is possible to measure distance with a reasonable degree of accuracy. To gauge the effects of distance on moves to a central point (Fig. 2.3a) we may simply draw equidistant bands of say one or five kilometres around the point, count up the numbers of moves within each band and graph the results from the frequency distribution as seen in Fig. 2.3b. The number of moves is plotted on the vertical axis against distance on the horizontal axis. This very simple approach may be refined by taking into account that the areas of the bands will increase from the migration centre outwards and that the numbers of possible origins (or destinations) of migrants will increase. A number of simple studies in various parts of the world have indeed shown that a clear inverse relationship between distance and the frequency of migration exists. A very clear-cut example for in- and out-migration to Surrey is shown in Fig. 2.4. Some of the most influential work has been carried out in Sweden, where good data sources have allowed the analysis of contemporary and historical patterns of movement and have shown the way in which the pattern of contacts has expanded over the last hundred years. For comparative purposes simple regression methods may be used to provide a statistical expression of the relationship. It may thus be shown how a particular town or city has expanded its migration field: that is, the area from which it draws migrants. An example of the effect of distance on migration is shown simply in Fig. 2.5. Here we see the way in which both in- and out-migration for the small town of Simrishamn on the south-east coast of Sweden at the start of the century is sensitive to the constraint of distance. The relationship is of course rarely smooth, for many factors such as the variable pull of urban centres intervene. This relationship of movement and distance (for example, in forms of non-permanent mobility like search for a marriage partner, seasonal migration, journey to work and leisure and other forms of circulation) has also been used as an indicator of the extent of people's information field, or knowledge of the world. It

19

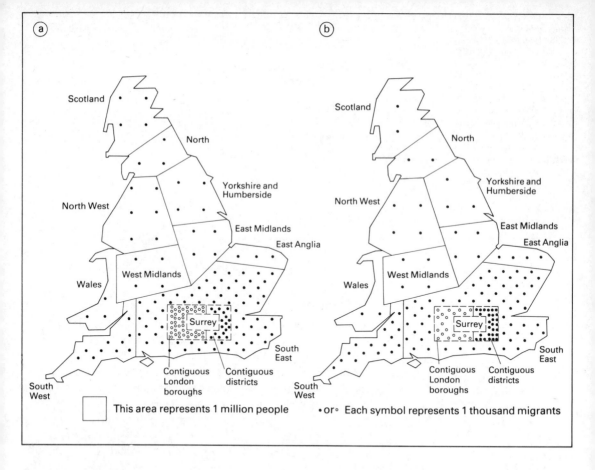

Fig 2.4 Migration between Surrey and the regions of Great Britain. Calculation of the origins of immigrants (a) and destinations of outmigrants (b) is based on the 1971 census question which recorded people's addresses five years previous to the census. The data show the similarity of origins and destinations and the strong effect of distance. *Source:* J. Craig (1981), 'Migration patterns of Surrey, Devon and South Yorkshire, *Population Trends* 23:18.

has been shown that the spatial extent of contacts is much influenced by factors such as race, age, sex and social class.

These simple relationships may be taken a step further. So far we have thought simply in terms of the distance covered from one place to another but the gravity model postulates that migration is related to the mass, or size, of the places as well as being inversely related to the distance between them. This may be put in the form of a simple equation:

$$M_{ij} = \frac{P_i P_j}{D_{ij}}$$

Where movement (M) between two places (i and j) is proportional to the product of their populations (P_i and P_j) and the distance between them (D_{ij}). Although this is based on Newton's Law of Universal Gravitation, of course, it is applicable to many cases of human movement. It is, after all, a reasonable proposition that migrant links with Birmingham, for example, are dominated either by adjacent areas (Coventry, Worcester, Kidderminster) or by more distant but populous areas (London, Manchester, Liverpool, Leeds or Newcastle). The number of people at origin or destination is clearly important in determining how many people are able to move and how many opportunities there are for migration to take place. Yet, these moves are likely to be limited by the difficulties and expense of travelling and by the fact that knowledge of distant places is likely to be less than of those nearby (Lee's intervening obstacles discussed earlier).

Fig 2.5 Migration to and from the town of Simrishamn, Sweden, 1900–04. Numbers of migrants are plotted for each 10-km distance band. There is a strong negative relationship between volume of movement and distance, particularly for in-migrants. Out-migrants are strongly attracted to other urban centres in the 70–90-km bands and to long-distance destinations more than 200 km away. *Source:* T. Hägerstrand (1962), 'Geographic measurements of migration, Swedish data', in J. Sutter (ed.), *Human displacements*, Entretiens de Monaco en Sciences Humaines, p. 77.

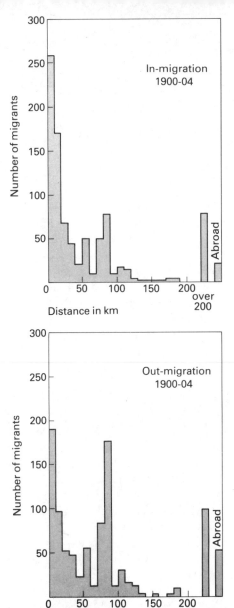

The gravity model may itself be modified to include more sophisticated measures of the influence of the origin or destination, for example using just the working population or particular age-groups according to the type of migration flow under study; or of distance, substituting distance by road, perhaps, or even time taken to travel, for a simple straight-line measure of distance.

It was this latter consideration that led Stouffer, an American social psychologist, to propose the idea of 'intervening opportunities'. That is, he tried to show that the number of migrants over a given distance was related to the number of opportunities at that distance and inversely related to the number of intervening opportunities. Huw Jones has recently summarised Stouffer's argument thus: 'that linear distance was less important a determinant of migration patterns than the nature of space; that distance should be regarded in socio-economic rather than

21

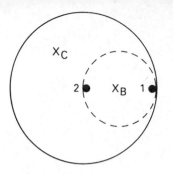

Fig 2.6 Simple representation of Stouffer's 'intervening opportunities' model. Migration between city 1 and city 2 may be influenced both by intervening opportunities within the circle XB and by the number of competing migrants in the area XC. *Source:* H. Jones (1981), p. 221.

geometric terms; and that because migration is costly, socially as well as financially, a mobile person will cease to move when he encounters an appropriate opportunity'. Likely 'opportunities' would include those provided by better housing, employment or environment. He further refined the model to suggest that not only would migration between city 1 and city 2 (Fig. 2.6) be determined by intervening opportunities (within the area XB in the figure) but also by the number of competing migrants (in the area XC) who might take up opportunities in city 2. The detailed application of this model to particular cases has shown its validity, for example in explaining 116 inter-city migration streams in the USA, while a study of Belgian movements showed that the model was suitable for analysing migration only *within* French and Flemish linguistic regions, emphasising the effect of cultural differences restraining migration between them.

More complex models—known as multiple regression models—have also been devised to try to explain particular migration flows. In these cases the dependent variable is some measure of migration between places, which is explained in terms of a number of independent or explanatory variables. These may be demographic, social or economic and may be varied according to the availability of information and its appropriateness for explaining a particular case. The most important variables include age structures, socio-economic status, previous experience of migration and environmental attractiveness of areas.

In reviewing spatial models of this type—both simple and more complex—two perhaps rather paradoxical observations may be made. First, that they sometimes ignore the wider economic and social environment in which migration operates and may tend towards the descriptive rather than the truly explanatory; and that they perhaps underestimate the role of the individual's attitudes and behaviour in determining migration patterns.

A systems approach

One further way of trying to make sense of the forces which lead to migration is the systems approach. The aim is to set migration in its economic and social context, as part of a system of interrelated elements. The best known example is that proposed by Akin Mabogunje in his study of rural–urban migration in Africa (Fig. 2.7), although the model could well be adapted to other cases, for example the period of industrialisation in the presently developed countries when rural–urban movement (see Chapter 4) was important. The advantage of the systems approach is that it does not see migration in over-simplified terms of cause and effect, but as a circular, interdependent and self-modifying

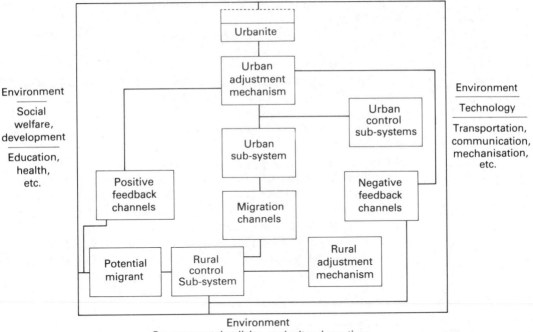

Environment
Economic conditions - wages, prices, consumer preferences,
degrees of commercialisation and industrial development

Urbanite

Urban adjustment mechanism

Urban control sub-systems

Urban sub-system

Environment

Social welfare, development

Education, health, etc.

Positive feedback channels

Negative feedback channels

Migration channels

Potential migrant

Rural control Sub-system

Rural adjustment mechanism

Environment

Technology

Transportation, communication, mechanisation, etc.

Environment
Governmental policies, agricultural practices,
marketing organisations, population movement, etc.

Fig 2.7 A systems approach to the study of migration from rural to urban areas. Migration is seen as a complex chain of interdependent forces at both origin and destination. The move from village to town is set within a particular economic, social and technological environment. *Source:* A. Mabogunje (1970), 'Systems approach to a theory of rural–urban migration', *Geographical Analysis* 2:22.

system. Changes in one part of the system may have a ripple effect in the whole.

Mabogunje's system is set within a particular environment (see Fig. 2.7): economic development is encouraging the break-up of isolation and self-sufficiency in rural communities. The rural economy is being integrated into the national economy with resulting changes in the countryside in wage and price levels and in levels of expectation and demand. The villager has become more aware of the greater range of opportunities the cities provide, both in jobs and in social welfare and education. The process of development may be affected too by government policies, in times both of colonial rule and of independence. It is, then, this general environment that determines the nature and extent of migration.

The migration system itself is made up of three elements. First, there is the potential migrant who is encouraged to leave the village by stimuli from the environment. Secondly, there are two control 'sub-systems', in which institutional forces, both rural and urban, affect the flow of migrants. In the rural case these may include the effect of the family and local community in restraining or encouraging mobility; in the urban case, the control sub-system determines, by means of the occupational and residential opportunities it offers, the degree to which migrants assimilate. Thirdly, there are adjustment mechanisms: once migration has occurred, adjustments are set in motion at both ends of the migration stream. At the rural end, out-migration may lead to increased income per head in the villages whilst also removing migrants from their families and communities. At the urban end, in-migration may involve the migrant in a wage-earning economy and in new social groups.

All systems contain a driving force, or energy, which in this case can be equated with the stimuli to move acting on the rural individual. In systems language, these stimuli may be seen as potential energy, while kinetic energy is released when the migration actually happens. This migration takes place in channels, with which are associated various questions of cost, distance and direction.

A final consideration in the system is the flow of information. A rural dweller's role in the system does not end with migration to the city: once installed, the migrant may maintain links with home, providing information—feed-back—of either a positive or a negative nature. Where it is negative, migration to the city may well slow down considerably, where it is positive regular migration flows will be established from a particular village to a particular city. Without information of this type, the system has no order or organisation; it tends towards randomness and disorder (or maximum entropy in systems language) which is reduced by the positive feedback of information.

The systems approach is thus useful in making us think of the decision to migrate as part of an interlocking series of causes and effects. Let us now turn to analyse separately several aspects of the process of migration.

Migration and economic factors

Turkish workers in a BMW car factory in West Germany. By 1980 there were some 624,000 Turkish workers in Germany. Despite some return migration in the 1970s, the original intention that foreign workers would be short-stay 'guests' has not been realised. The importance of the foreign population in West Germany is likely to grow.

Ravenstein's early notion of the importance of economic factors in determining migration was expressed by him as follows: 'Bad or oppressive laws, heavy taxation, an unattractive climate, uncongenial social surroundings, and even compulsion (slave trade, transportation) all have produced and are still producing currents of migration, but none of these currents can compare in volume with that which arises from the desire inherent in most men to 'better' themselves in material respects.' Similarly, we have seen in the idea of the mobility transition that economic development has consequences for the volume and type of

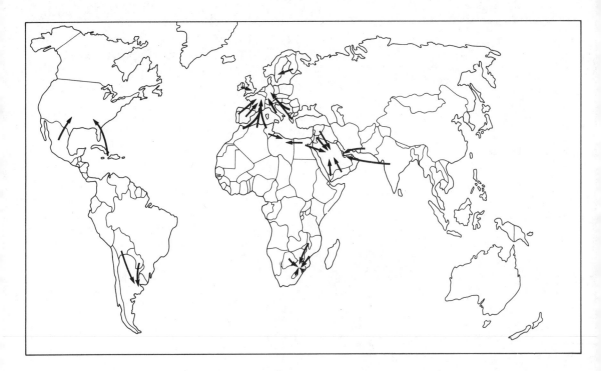

Fig 2.8 Major international flows of migrant workers within regional labour markets in the 1970s. The cases highlighted here emphasise the flow from 'periphery' to 'core', for example from southern Europe and North Africa to Western Europe or from Mexico and the Caribbean to the USA. *Source:* H. Jones (1981) p. 267.

mobility. It is a theme which underlies, and is treated in more detail in, Chapters 3 and 4 of this book.

At the broadest scale, migration has been seen as part of the development of capitalism, the economic system which characterises the Western world. Thus, migration is one aspect of the divisions which exist between core and periphery, between cities and the countryside and between metropolitan and colonial areas. The city grows by importing labour from the countryside, and developed core regions or countries use underdeveloped regions or colonies for supplies both of raw materials and of labour. The economic fortunes of origin and destination are thus inextricably linked. In addition, the migrant is often severely disadvantaged socially in the core area because he or she tends to take jobs at the bottom of the socio-economic spectrum and may belong to a distinctive ethnic or racial group. This type of broad-brush approach provides an all-embracing set of relationships between economy, society and regional development which allow us to look at the historical evolution and contemporary form of world society, and migration is but one example of these wider processes. A classic case which illustrates this approach is the slave trade, where forced migration on a large scale (for example from Africa to the Caribbean and the southern USA) allowed an intensive agricultural development which in turn aided growth at the European core. Equally, development within the European core itself was aided by the migration, first during the nineteenth and early twentieth century, of peasants from countryside to town (see Chapter 4), in countries like France or Germany; and latterly the importation of labour from the Third World and other peripheral states, from the Caribbean and southern Asia to Britain, from North Africa to France, from Greece and Turkey to Germany (see Chapter 3). We may see the major international world flows (Fig. 2.8) in this light, while internal flows in, for example, Tunisia are really part of the same process, at the internal level, of

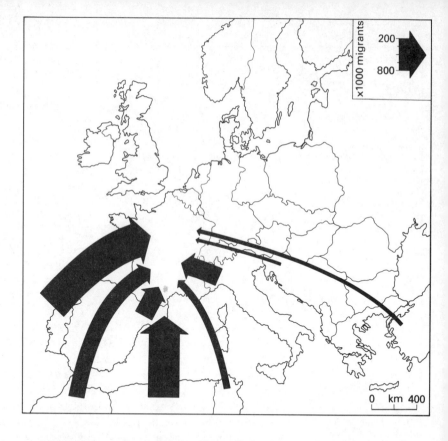

Fig 2.9 Origins of major foreign groups resident in France in 1982. A long history of immigration culminated in particularly marked inflows in the 1950s and 1960s. A total foreign population of 4.2 million in 1982 was made up of immigrants from Portugal, Spain and Italy and from North Africa, with smaller numbers from Greece and Turkey. *Source:* based on data from OECD (1983) *Continuous reporting system on migration (SOPEMI) 1982* (Paris), p. 36.

x1000 migrants

200

800

0   km   400

transfer of labour from countryside to town, from periphery to core as for France at the international scale (Fig. 2.9).

A rather different approach to the economics of migration is that which sees migration in terms of costs and benefits and which measures flows in relation to such factors as wages, employment opportunities and their regional inequalities forming part of a mass of 'push' and 'pull' factors. Woods has commented that 'at its simplest this theory specifies that potential migrants respond to differentials in real income levels which they adjust to allow for the costs associated with migration. They migrate with the intention of maximising personal economic gains and do so as long as expected net gains are substantial enough.' At a national scale, various studies have shown the relationship between, for example, migration and the number of vacant jobs. Fig. 2.10 illustrates this for Sweden and Finland. A common free labour market was introduced in Scandinavia in 1954 but the main factors producing movement from Finland to Sweden from the middle 1960s were twofold: in Finland jobs were fewer because of decline in some sectors of the economy and because many youngsters were competing in the job market; and this coincided with heavy demand for labour in the Swedish economy. In the years 1969 and 1970 alone some 80,000 Finns, or 1.8% of the population, left for Sweden and this was linked also to the extra opportunities created after 1967 when Sweden restricted immigration from non-Scandinavian states. Information about available opportunities is mainly spread by letters, telephone calls and person-to-person contacts with relatives and friends who give potential migrants a fairly sensitive appreciation of opportunities in Sweden. During the 1970s migration slowed as recession made itself felt (see Chapter 3).

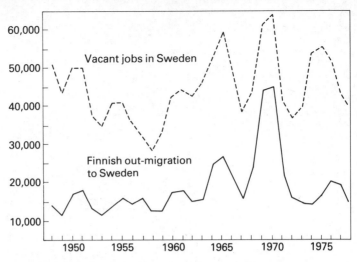

Fig 2.10 Correlation between Finnish migration to Sweden and the number of vacant jobs in Sweden 1948-78. From the mid-1960s a strong demand for labour in the Swedish economy was matched by migration from Finland, the latter showing sensitivity to cyclical changes in the former. *Source:* L.-E. Borgegård and N. Häggström (1981), 'Migration decisions in theory and practice: Finland to Sweden after 1945', in J.W. Webb, A. Naukkarinen and L.A. Kosiński (eds.), p. 127.

Similar examples indicate how West Indian migration to Britain before 1962, when restrictions were first imposed, was clearly related to the need for unskilled labour in Britain, and fluctuations in migration are related to fluctuations in employment vacancies, with a certain lag for transatlantic flow of information to take place. Equally, work on transatlantic migration from Britain to the USA in the nineteenth century has shown its relationship with fluctuations in trade. Before the First World War, trade cycles were so far out of phase that when the American economy was in boom, the West European one was in recession, thus creating ideal 'push' and 'pull' factors for migration.

We could of course also find frequent examples at the regional level of the impact of employment opportunities, wages and other inequalities on migration flow. The very nature of a person's occupation has an important effect on his likely mobility. Some occupations, like farming, often imply a certain degree of stability, whilst promotion and advancement in others may require the individual to change residence quite frequently. Equally, we should at this point mention in passing the role of government policy in this field, which may do much either to foster or restrict labour migration, both international and internal. These points are developed in Chapter 6. For the theme of this book it is certainly true that there are interlocking and reciprocal links between migration and the changing geography of the economy.

Migration and social factors

Distinct from, but not unrelated to, economic factors underlying migration are those concerned more specifically with social patterns, in relation both to causes and effects of movement. Under social causes, we may include the extreme cases of social oppression and political control which underlie, for example, certain international migrations discussed in the next chapter or the evolution of migration policies treated in Chapter 6. We may also mention a number of factors concerned with the nature of a particular society as a whole and the individuals within it which shape migration flows. These include the provision of housing and education, which may have a significant influence on a family's ability to move; the influence of education itself on an individual's social and occupational progress and therefore his likelihood of moving; the influence of different stages of the life cycle (see below) and its resulting effect on the age and

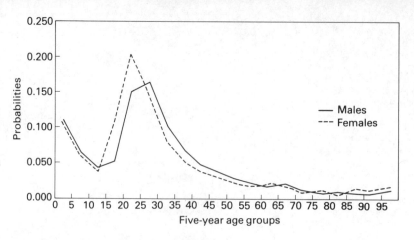

Fig 2.11 Age-specific probability of migrating, Sweden 1966. Young adults between the ages of 20 and 30 are highly mobile. The peak for women in their early twenties reflects a tendency to move on marriage, whilst the small peaks between 60 and 65 for women and 65 and 70 for men indicate retirement moves. The general pattern shown here is valid for many other countries and groups. *Source:* R.I. Woods (1979), p. 171.

sex pattern of migrants; and the effect of migrants' ethnic and racial characteristics, as well as those of language or religion, on their pattern of settlement and adaptation. The selectivity which these factors imply reflects not only the causes of migration but its consequences for the destination areas too: migration streams selected by age or sex or race have done much to transform the social geography of the city, for example (Chapter 5).

Several of these aspects will come up in the following chapters but let us take one example—the idea of the 'life cycle' and its effects on mobility. By the term 'life cycle' we mean the successive stages between birth and death with which particular forms of mobility may be associated. Important stages in the life cycle include leaving home for education or to find employment; getting married; rearing a family; and retirement. Within the period of family formation, for example, there may be direct relationships with mobility. A young married couple with no children will have limited space requirements and a modest income and may live centrally. Child-bearing brings a demand for a larger house and better environment, with perhaps a move to the suburbs and a period of stability. When the children have left home, the parents may choose to move to a smaller house or back into the city or retire to the country or seaside. Finally, perhaps with the death of one partner, the remaining person may move into sheltered accommodation or go to live with a relative. If we consider Fig. 2.11 for Sweden we can see that the period of greatest mobility is between the ages of 20 and 30. The higher peak for females shows their greater tendency to move on marriage; the peak for children under five shows that couples retain an ability to move so long as children are below school age; and the small peaks just after 60 for women and 65 for men show the effects of retirement. The detailed links between life cycle and the age structures of particular areas are shown in Fig. 2.12. On the left are shown alternative routes through a household life cycle, the dotted line indicating the fact that older households may occasionally move to join households formed by their children. On the right are the corresponding effects on age patterns: at stage 2, for example, the newly formed household contributes to the 20-30-year category most while at stage 7 the contribution of widows and widowers is especially to the age-group over 65.

The selectivity of migration by age and sex means that some migrant flows can lead to sharp differences between the sexes and contribute dramatically to the host populations. Two cases illustrate these different

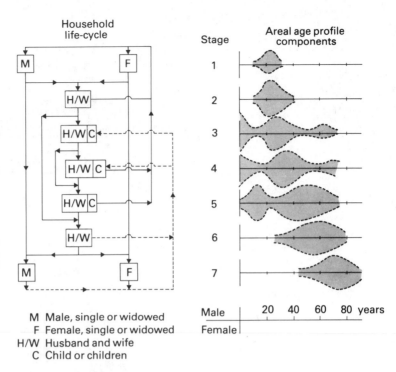

Fig 2.12 Household life-cycles and the age profile of areas. On the left is shown the formation of the household and its transition through child-rearing to eventual widow-hood. On the right, the effect on age distributions is shown, the couple in stage 2 moving through to old age in stages 6 and 7, accompanied by young or adolescent children and occasionally by aged parents. Each stage may be associated with particular forms of residential mobility and immobility. *Source:* B.T. Robson (1973), 'A view on the urban scene', in M. Chisholm and B. Rodgers (eds.) *Studies in human geography* (Heinemann, London), p. 229.

M Male, single or widowed
F Female, single or widowed
H/W Husband and wife
C Child or children

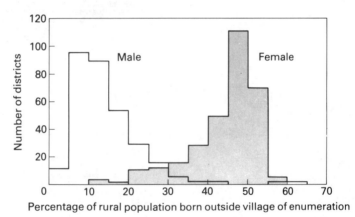

Fig 2.13 Village in-migration in India for men and women, 1961. Women are markedly more likely to be born outside the village where they live, mainly because of migration for marriage. A similar pattern may be found in many other countries. *Source:* M.J. Libbee and D.E. Sopher (1975), 'Marriage migration in rural India', in L.A. Kósiński and R.M. Prothero (eds.), p. 350.

points. Fig. 2.13 shows for rural India the greater mobility of women, particularly associated with marriage: many districts recorded between 55% and 65% of women born outside the village compared to perhaps 5–15% of men. In a very different case, for Swedish migrants to America, Fig. 2.14 shows the way in which migrant selectivity shaped the structure of the new community of Swedes in Worcester, Massachusetts in the later nineteenth century. If we compare the age pyramids for that area with Sweden as a whole we see that men in the age-group 20–34 predominate, there are fewer women and far fewer children: this reflects the fact that Swedes had only just begun to settle in the area and that the industrial labour market in Worcester was dominated by the iron industry. A contemporary example of this effect is given in Fig. 3.7 for France; while Table 2.1 shows the predominance of males in migration flows to selected countries of West Africa.

29

Fig 2.14 Sex and age distribution of Swedes in (a) Worcester, Massachusetts and (b)Sweden, 1880. The strong selectivity by age is shown by the over-representation of age-groups 20–34 in (a), particularly amongst males. Such an age-pyramid is typical of many groups soon after immigration. *Source:* H. Runblom and H. Norman (eds.)(1976), p. 280.

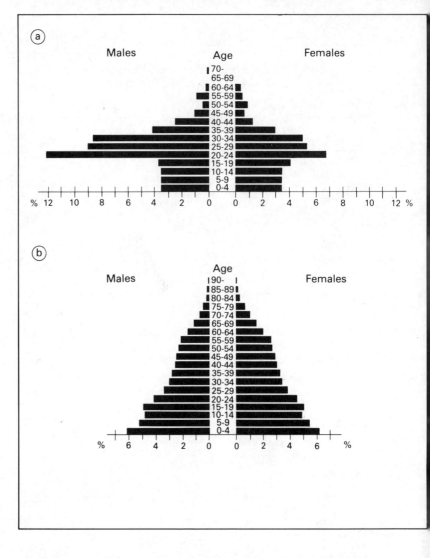

Table 2.1   Sex ratios of migrants and total population of working age, around 1975, for selected West African countries. *Source:* Zachariah and Condé (1981), p. 46.

Country	Males per 100 females	
	Immigrants	Total population
Gambia	181	104
Ghana	166	96
Ivory Coast	177	110
Liberia	164	103
Senegal	119	84
Sierra Leone	187	97

Migration and individual behaviour

A final set of factors which we should not neglect specifically recognises the importance of the individual and the way in which he or she reaches the decision to move. Groups are made up of individuals each with particular attitudes, attributes and access to information about the world around him or her which lead to a certain form of behaviour. Identical economic or social factors can have different effects according to the way individuals perceive them. Thus the positive, negative and neutral factors identified at origin and destination by Lee may be differently viewed by individuals and lead to different decisions about migration. We should bear in mind that the decision to move is an important one for the individual, often involving a break with family and community ties and involving effort and expense. Julian Wolpert's work on migrant behaviour has emphasised that behaviour is rational only up to a certain point and is influenced by social, economic and physical environments. A central idea is that of 'place utility' or the degree to which an individual is satisfied or dissatisfied with a place. An individual's place utility for his present residence has a strong degree of certainty about it, based on familiarity, but is much more speculative for other places.

The idea of an individual's information about the world around him is crucial to understanding behaviour. The procedure by which an individual gathers such information is guided by the extent and content of his 'information field' or the set of places about which he has knowledge. This often shows a simple relationship with distance, where knowledge is greatest of the area immediately adjacent and lessens with increasing distance, fostered by the intensity of contacts at work or amongst family and friends within the local community of village or city neighbourhood. Knowledge about distant locations may be highly selective and may again be influenced by contacts with family and friends, by recollections of personal visits, letters from past migrants, or by books, newspapers and broadcasts: the idea of 'chain migration' is based on the fact that information about a particular place is passed back by those who are already installed as migrants, and so influences the movement of other individuals. We have seen this element built into the systems model and we shall see in subsequent chapters how it may influence, for example, the destinations of international migrants and in particular the way in which immigrant groups in cities retain contact with areas of origin.

It is important to remember that both the quantity and quality of information available to the individual will be limited and biased and that the decision-making process is based not on the objective attributes of a particular area but on the individual's perceptions of those attributes. Various attempts have been made to measure the individual's view of the world, to draw his or her 'mental map'. Two approaches are particularly interesting. The first determines, perhaps by means of a questionnaire, how an individual sees the form of the city, for example, around him. Studies, particularly in North America, show how distorted is the individual's image, conditioned by factors such as age, occupation, social class and race, and influenced by physical obstacles (for example, rivers or major roadways), transport systems and well-known city landmarks. Clearly the West Indian resident of Brixton has a rather different view of London and its geography, though not necessarily a more distorted one, from that of the stockbroker of Belgravia.

Secondly, we may study people's preferences, that is to say determine, again by questionnaire, individual perceptions of the desirability of living in particular areas. One well-known study (Fig. 2.15a and b) questioned several hundred school-leavers at 23 schools all over Britain. They were given county maps of Britain and were asked to record directly on the map their personal preferences for residence. If we take the examples of schools in Bristol and Inverness we find quite distinct patterns. In the first case, there is a strong preference for the area immediately around, for Devon and Cornwall and for most of the south coast. While preferences

Fig 2.15 Mental preference images in Britain. A sample of school leavers in (a) Bristol and (b) Inverness were asked to identify their preferred places of residence. The patterns are distinct, yet both showed a preference for their local areas and for parts of south-eastern and south-western England. *Source:* P. Gould and R. White (1974), *Mental maps* (Penguin, Harmondsworth), pp. 71, 57.

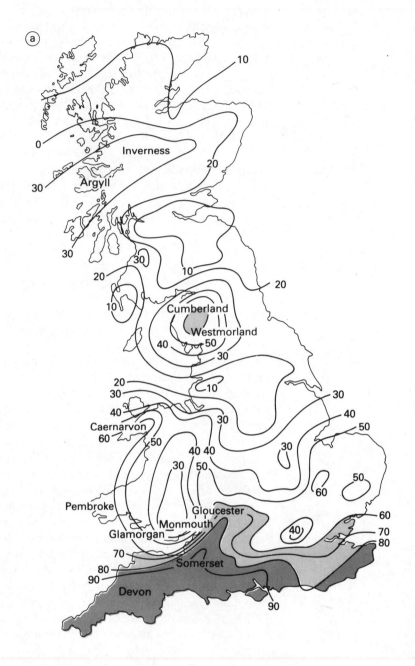

diminish rapidly as we move further north, there are areas of high desirability, for example Cambridge, Hereford or the Lake District. In the Inverness case, there is also a strong preference for adjacent areas and indeed a strong Scottishness to the pattern (other peaks including Edinburgh and Ayr). The Scots view of much of England (and almost all of Wales) is unfavourable, except for parts of the South West, South East and East Anglia.

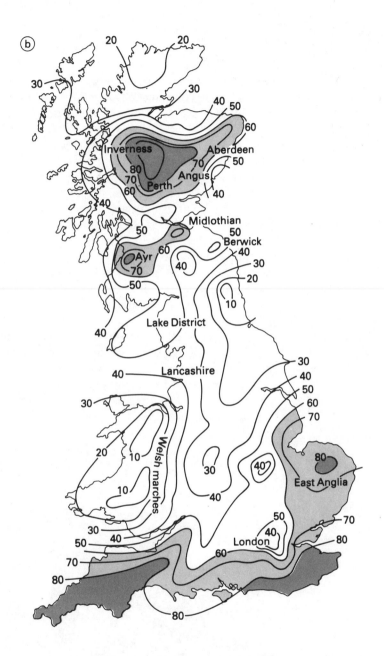

The purpose of such surveys is not, of course, to act as an accurate predictor of migration trends but to serve as a reminder that individual views of the world do not necessarily accord with the contours of the geographer's 'objective' map. Personal preferences are curtailed by the economic and social factors outlined above: we should all like to while away a happy existence in the Lake District, but we do not all have the opportunity to do so.

3 International migration

Introduction

Few aspects of migration produce such evident and fundamental effects as international movements. Often of great historical importance, international migrations have an immense, if often overlooked, impact on the diffusion of culture, on economic development and on social change. From prehistoric migrations, through slavery, mass migrations to the 'New World' in the nineteenth and early twentieth centuries, post-1945 immigration to western European cities, and even the 'brain drain'—all have left remarkable effects on areas of destination, as they have to a lesser extent on areas of origin. Whole nations—the USA, Australia, New Zealand, the Caribbean islands and parts of Latin America—have been largely fashioned from immigrants. At a more local scale, the social structure of individual cities is often shaped as much by international movements as by migration within the state concerned. Moreover, as Chapter 6 emphasises, the growing need to regulate movement between nations has given rise to immensely complex, and often bitterly disputed, policies.

This chapter seeks to emphasise a number of points: the need to remember the broad influences of international movements and their immense variety both historically and geographically; the complex relationship between economic and social causes and effects; and, somewhat conversely, the need to remember that however large the flow, it is made up of individuals from whose experience we may learn a great deal.

Victims of political turmoil in the aftermath of war, large numbers of refugees from Vietnam in the late 1970s received world-wide attention They became known as the 'boat people' because fragile craft like this offered their main means of escape from political repression. This group survived; many were less fortunate.

Definitions

The very term international migration is of course something of an arbitrary notion. In many cases, international movements are distinctive and worth treating in their own right. Yet the mere act of crossing a national boundary, though a useful basis for definition, does not in itself imply a difference in economic or social cause. In the case of western Europe, for example, it may be useful to see the movement of Italian or Spanish workers to French cities in much the same light as rural–urban movements of French peasants. The simple crossing of a boundary, though, provides a most appropriate framework for data collection. In this, as in other fields of migration study, data are incomplete and unreliable. For past periods, there are enormous gaps in our knowledge occasioned by the fact that for prehistoric movements or for slavery, no formal records were kept. Yet even for contemporary movements the existence of illegal and clandestine migration makes analysis frequently problematical.

Following our definitions in Chapters 1 and 2, international migration may generally be taken to include permanent changes of residence from one country to another and, in addition, temporary movements such as seasonal migration. Further, at the international more than at any other level, perhaps, the division between free and forced migration is crucial.

Causes

In a recent study of migration and European economic development in the nineteenth century Milward and Saul remarked that the

> 'key question is one of motive, for emigration was rarely accomplished without anguish and hardship and the benefits were most often reaped only by the succeeding generations. Some went because the economic situation at home was hopeless, some because the chance of getting land somewhere offered greater opportunities to them and their families. Some sought new opportunities, some went to avoid change... Some wanted to escape military service, some disliked taxes and the insolence of officials. Some went overseas in search of greater political and religious freedom... some were paid to go: some went for the adventure... At times it became almost a fever, an irrational frenzy.'

This lengthy quotation gives a key to the fact that international migrations are usually determined by the complex interplay of 'push' factors at origin and 'pull' factors at destination, except of course in the simpler case of forced migrations. For forced migrations, reasons vary too. In the case of slavery, coercion was practised for purely commercial ends, by slave-traders with government encouragement or acquiescence. In the seventeenth and eighteenth centuries, it has been estimated, some 7.7 million slaves were transported from West Africa to the Americas. Governments and war play a dominant role in determining forced migrations and we should not underestimate the numbers involved. Further examples include Huguenot refugees to Britain in the eighteenth century, the expulsion of Jews from Germany between the World Wars, or modern refugee movements such as the expulsion of Asians from East Africa in the 1960s, the 'boat people' from Vietnam in the late 1970s or the expulsion of migrants from Nigeria in 1983. The Second World War itself provoked a massive shifting of people, some permanently, some

Ford Madox Brown's *The Last of England* (1885) has become a well-known image of the emigrant's lot. This couple — with their child's hand just visible — was bound for Australia.

Fig 3.1 Migrations in Europe between 1944 and 1951. The aftermath of war and new political regimes and boundaries provoked complex population movements. Particularly marked is the movement into West Germany of ethnic Germans from Poland, Czechoslovakia and Hungary and of many other refugees, who totalled some 8 million by 1950. *Source:* J. Salt and H. Clout (eds.)(1976), p. 22, after J.O. Broek and J.W. Webb (1968), *A geography of mankind* (McGraw Hill, New York).

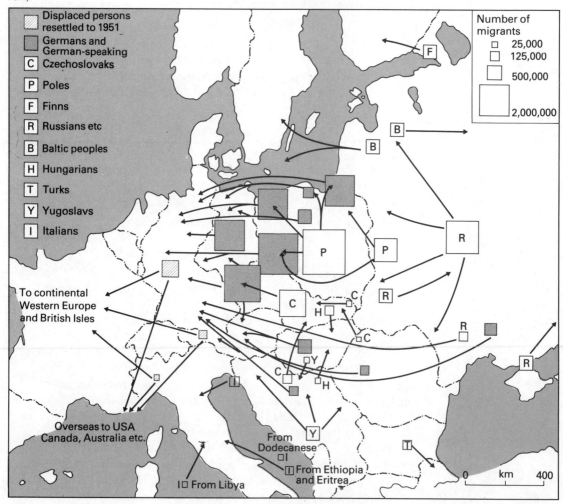

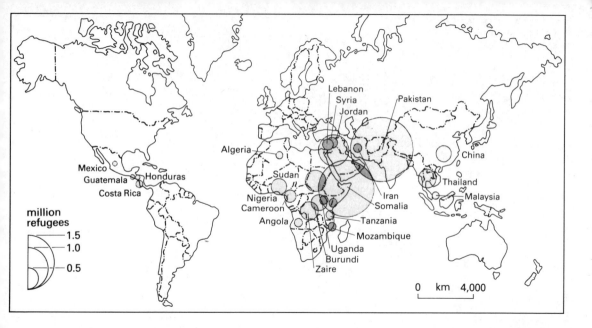

million
refugees

—1.5

—1.0

—0.5

0   km   4,000

Fig 3.2 Refugees in the world, 1980. The United Nations' High Commission for Refugees (UNHCR) estimates the total at 12 million. There are large numbers in the Middle East and in Africa and Asia, victims of war and persecution. *Source:* W.T. Gould (1982), p. 496.

temporarily. Many of these movements are difficult to measure, but one estimate puts at 25 million the number of people who moved during and immediately after the Second World War, especially in east-central Europe (see Fig. 3.1). Indeed, many migrations in twentieth-century Europe were inspired by political events: the First World War led to a movement of nearly 8 million people and smaller moves followed, for example, the Spanish Civil War, the establishment of Fascism in Italy or the anti-Jewish policies in 1930s Germany. One of the most publicised examples has been the flight of refugees to West Germany after 1945. By 1950 West Germany had almost 8 million refugees, mainly from the East. The flow from East Germany in particular continued up to the building of the Berlin Wall in 1961: between 1950 and 1961 some 3 million crossed from East Germany to the West, very few going in the other direction. Later movements of refugees of a totally different nature included the repatriation of Dutch from Indonesia or the return of almost a million Frenchmen, *pieds-noirs*, from Algeria in the early 1960s. Current estimates of the numbers of refugees in the world are instructive. The United Nations High Commissioner for Refugees (UNHCR) puts the total for 1981 at 12 million. As Fig. 3.2 shows, the majority are found in Third World countries, often in the poorest states in Africa (for example Tanzania or Somalia) and Asia (Pakistan and Thailand), having fled from war or persecution on religious or economic grounds.

Economic causes of movement are in many cases predominant. Mobility of labour is an essential part of the evolution and functioning of Western capitalism. Strong economic forces at origin and destination have shaped in large measure, for example, emigration from Europe to the United States or contemporary migration from the southern and eastern European periphery to the 'core' countries of Germany, France, Switzerland and the Low Countries. A strong demand for labour usually finds a source and it should not be forgotten that the effect of chain migration (see Chapter 1) producing an almost habitual movement often blurs the original motive. We should also remember that perceived economic opportunity—what people think a destination offers—may be

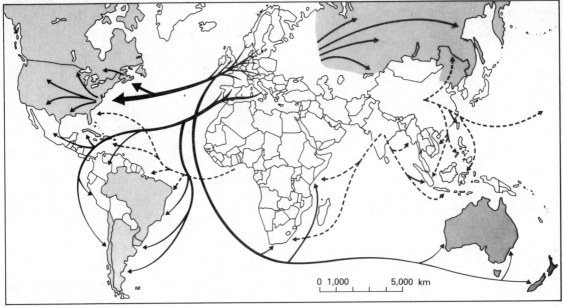

Migration of European population   - - → Migration of non-European populations

Countries where more than half of the population is descended from immigrants in recent centuries

Fig 3.3 Principal international migrations in recent centuries. Migration has had a powerful global effect, particularly in North America, Australia, parts of Latin America and the Soviet Union. European migrations in the nineteenth century dominate, but other major flows include the slave trade from West Africa and a variety of movements from India and China. *Source:* D. Noin (1979), *Géographie de la population,* (Masson, Paris) p. 85.

as important as the economic facts, since migration as we have noted is frequently a product of very individual motivations. Supplementary causes are a host of factors which we may loosely term 'social', again operating as both 'push' and 'pull' factors at origin and destination. Examples include the general desire for social betterment associated with better jobs, housing and social facilities at destination or the feeling of social oppression at origin because of discrimination on grounds of race, or religion.

Effects

International migrations may have effects of the most profound sort, both on areas of origin of migrants and on the areas they go to. Fig. 3.3 shows the major world movements and hints at the geographically widespread nature of their effects. Effects may be of several types: cultural, demographic, economic and social.

Fig. 3.3 shows particularly the cultural effects at a world scale which, in our detailed analysis of contemporary movements, are often forgotten. The major of these, developed in detail in the next section, is the expansion of European influence through colonisation: the USA, Australia and New Zealand, parts of Latin America, have been dominated by European influence, while colonial influence has made itself felt too in many parts of Africa and the Far East. In addition, the map also points to the movement of Asians to East Africa, resulting for example in the eventual notorious expulsion of Asians from Uganda in the 1970s; to the eastward colonising movement of Russians; and to a variety of movements in the Far East, from China and elsewhere. Lastly the map shows the movement of black Africans, through the slave trade, to the Americas. Of all these examples, the United States are perhaps the best illustration of the direct cultural effects of migration. Yet smaller-scale examples can be no less impressive: in the Caribbean islands of the French West Indies, Guadeloupe and Martinique, an original Amerindian population has been swamped by progressive waves of migration of white French settlers, transient white administrators, black slaves, Indian indentured labour and immigrants from neighbouring British islands. The outcome of decades of mixed marriages is to produce a population of astonishing variety. Cultural tensions may also be a direct product of migration. In Assam in north-east India in the early 1980s, for example, violent conflict was produced between local Hindus and Muslim immigrants from Bangladesh.

The demographic effects of movement on areas of destination are usually decisive only if migration is of the colonising, pioneering type. Certainly in the USA (Table 3.5) there were periods when immigration accounted for over 40% of population growth. In other cases, demographic effects may also be crucial, especially where, as is often the case, the emigrants are young adults and, therefore, those most likely to bear children. The classic case of effects on areas of origin is Ireland, where, during the nineteenth century, mass emigration contributed to reducing the total population from 6.5 million in 1831-41 to under 3 million by the decade after the First World War, and to producing a severely distorted age and sex structure. In other parts of western Europe too, mass migration in the nineteenth century had the effect of relieving over-population and demographic pressure in the countryside, for example in southern Italy. Contemporary Europe presents a different picture: recent immigration in the post-war years has been a significant contributor to population growth, especially in the 1960s and 1970s when fertility was declining rapidly amongst the home population. For England and Wales and for London, Table 3.1 shows the proportion of all live births to mothers born in New Commonwealth countries and Pakistan; in

Table 3.1 Births to women whose own birthplace was in the New Commonwealth or Pakistan, for England and Wales and Greater London. *Source:* GLC (1982), *Social and economic characteristics of ethnic minorities in Greater London.* Statistical Series II, Table 16.

	England and Wales (No.)	(%)	Greater London (No.)	(%)
1970	46,039	5.9	19,870	17.1
1975	39,965	6.6	16,675	19.4
1980	53,478	8.5	21.294	22.6

other north-west European countries immigrants contribute similarly. France in particular is a good, if somewhat peculiar, example of this relationship. Never a country of mass emigration, France has frequently relied upon immigration to fuel a generally lagging rate of population growth. In the period 1921–30, for example, net immigration accounted for over 75% of population increase. Similarly a great post-war surge of immigration, especially from the late 1950s, has led to there being over 4 million foreigners by the end of the 1970s: they represent 7% of the population but contribute 11.4% of children born in 1978. This is because the families moving from North Africa or Portugal, for example, tend to retain at least for a while the higher fertility associated with their area of origin, which offsets the fact that many of the immigrants are single men.

A recent study of nine West African countries (Ghana, Liberia, Sierra Leone, the Gambia, Ivory Coast, Upper Volta, Senegal, Mali and Togo), whose total population stood at 40 million in 1975, showed that the range of population growth rates was from 1.7% per annum for Upper Volta to 6.0% for Ivory Coast. This variation was, however, due much more to migration than to natural increase, as rates of birth and death were very similar from country to country. The total number of foreign nationals living in these countries was 2.8 million in 1975, or 7% of the total population. In Ivory Coast alone, there were 1.43 million foreign nationals, mainly from Upper Volta, Mali and Guinea out of a total population of about 6.7 million in 1975.

Economic effects are often less clear-cut and open to various interpretations for countries of origin and destination. For forced movements, the effect is unpredictable. Post-war refugees from eastern to western Europe may have contributed to economic recovery. The expulsion of 20,000 Ugandan Asians to Britain in 1972 had a debilitating effect on Ugandan commerce but did not produce the predicted problems of integration into British society. The expulsion of Jews at various periods, for example from Fascist regimes in Europe in the 1930s, was to the benefit of many aspects of scientific and industrial life in the areas of reception. For voluntary migrations, since economic causes are so important, it is not surprising that economic effects are frequently marked. For the areas of origin, these effects are much disputed. One point of view argues that migration, by removing excess population, stimulates the economy; another that it drains off the younger, more active and sometimes better-educated section of the population. The Italian countryside in the nineteenth century was overpopulated, the Scandinavian countries much less so, and yet both produced major outflows of migrants.

The economic effect of migrant remittances home is also much discussed. The quantity of money sent home—by Europeans in the USA a century ago, or by southern Europeans in north-west Europe today—is frequently very great. As Table 3.2 shows, in contemporary Europe remittances may form a very large part of overseas earnings. On the face of it, this may seem to be a good thing, bringing sorely needed cash into the family, into peasant or village society. Some argue, though, that it has a destructive effect, destroying individualism and self-reliance at home. Much of the money is not used on investment in, say, better farm machinery but in buying consumer goods or better housing. Some may be used for the upkeep of children left behind, on financing relatives who want to emigrate or on education, which itself increases the propensity to move. The effect of the migrant returning home is similarly open to different interpretations. He may return with new skills and experience which will aid in the development of a primitive industrial economy. A recent study of Algeria, on the other hand, showed that while workers returning from France would have experience in building and construction, they would in fact be needed in chemicals, hydrocarbons and textile industries.

Table 3.2 Transfer of funds home by emigrants, 1973.
Source: Power (1979), 139.

	Remittances ($m.)	Commodity exports ($m.)	Remittances as % of export earnings
Turkey	1,183	1,310	90
Greece	735	1,454	51
Yugoslavia	1,398	3,025	46
Spain	1,185	5,178	23
Portugal	1,025	1,750	59

Economic benefits to countries of destination are more clear-cut. The economic development of the USA, Australia or New Zealand has been much enhanced by immigration. In western Europe, post-war immigration responded to a demand for labour and, especially where the immigration flow could be turned off like a tap by the application of selective controls, it has worked greatly to the benefit of the country concerned. Some countries have made ruthless use of immigrants, encouraging the migration of single, male, temporary migrants rather than families. If immigrants can be shipped in in times of economic boom and out again in times of economic recession then all is well. Currently in the late 1970s and early 1980s, in a time of recession, we see most north-west European countries tightening up immigration control and in certain cases encouraging repatriation. Migrant workers are, of course, particularly useful commercially in the place they fill in the occupational spectrum; usually they take the worst jobs, at the bottom of the pile, that native workers no longer do, whether in industry or in services. In Great Britain a high proportion of certain service industries is staffed by immigrants: London Underground workers and nurses are examples.

This last point gives us a clue also to the array of social effects associated with international movements. We should not lose sight of the fact that for many of the individuals concerned migration was an occasion for immense grief, breaking up of families, severing deeply cherished ties. The picture by Ford Madox Brown, *The last of England* (1855) well summarises these emotions in the case of a migrant group bound for Australia. Despite the fact that we classify many migrants as 'voluntary', this is a misnomer since, although they were not directly forced by the state, they may not in fact have wanted to go. A recent writer remarked perceptively 'that in the end future generations may have benefited from the move very greatly in an economic sense makes no difference to the tragedy experienced by the generation that went'. Letters home from migrants to Australia or the USA for example have

The expulsion of hundreds of thousands of Ghanaians from Nigeria in January 1983 caused chaos, as this scene on the border between Ghana and Togo shows. Estimates put the number of migrants involved at up to two million.

Table 3.3 Unemployment in Greater London, 1979–81. *Source:* GLC (1982), *Social and economic characteristics of ethnic minorities in Greater London,* Statistical Series II, Table 43.

Region of origin	Males			Females			Total
	May 1979	Nov. 1981	% increase	May 1979	Nov. 1981	% increase	% increase
Total	102,654	239,072	133	31,396	90,930	190	146
Other than New Commonwealth	90,868	207,880	129	26,934	76,903	186	142
New Commonwealth* and Pakistan	11,786	31,192	165	4,462	14,027	214	178

*Includes Africa, West Indies, India, Bangladesh and others.

occasionally been preserved and add much to our knowledge of the migrant experience. For the areas of origin, social effects may perhaps be beneficial if excess population is creamed off and yet, more frequently, the effect is to upset family ties and create imbalance within the community left behind. This is particularly true of contemporary labour migrations where there is a predominance of single men.

For the countries of destination, an obvious social effect is that resulting from the mixing of races, particularly in urban areas. In all migrations, a period of adaptation and acculturation is necessary before anything resembling assimilation is achieved. The difficulties are frequently in proportion to the distinctiveness of the migrants: as Chapter 5 shows, colour, language, religion and occupation are all powerful determinants of segregation. The social geography of many parts of the modern city is directly attributable to migration. In Britain, the influx of 'New Commonwealth' migrants—principally from India, Pakistan and the Caribbean—and the need to guard against prejudice gave rise first to the Race Relations Board in 1965, the Community Relations Commission in 1968 and their successor the Commission for Racial Equality in 1976. Table 3.3 reveals one aspect of disadvantage: immigrants and their children from New Commonwealth countries have been more prone than average to the ravages of unemployment. The young are more affected than the old; women more than men; certain ethnic groups more than others.

Migration to the United States

'Give me your tired, your poor, your huddled masses yearning to breathe free...'

(Inscription on the Statue of Liberty)

The peopling of what are now the United States of America provides perhaps the most fascinating of all examples of international migrations. The permanent more or less voluntary migration out of Europe in the nineteenth and early twentieth centuries was one of the largest human migrations in history. The vast majority of European migrants went to the USA, creating a huge 'melting-pot' of cultures, languages and religions although millions of others went to people the Asiatic parts of the present USSR, Argentina, Canada and Australia. In the period 1846–1932 some 18 million people left Great Britain and Ireland and some 10 million left Italy for a variety of destinations. The United States during the century 1830–1932 alone received some 24 million immigrants. Migrants and their offspring were thus crucial in securing the increase of the population of the USA from 1.2 million in 1750 to 106 million in 1920

Table 3.4 Average annual overseas emigration from Europe for selected dates and for 'old' and 'new' groups. *Source:* D. Kirk (1946), *Europe's population in the inter-war years* (Gordan and Breach, New York), p. 279.

Period	'Old' migration* (000s)	'New' migration** (000s)
1846–50	254.3	2.3
1866–70	308.4	37.4
1886–90	407.2	330.5
1906–10	322.3	1,114.3
1926–30	253.5	302.2

* British Isles, Germany, Norway, Sweden, Denmark, France, Switzerland, Low Countries.

** Italy, Austria, Hungary, Czechoslovakia, Russia, Poland, Lithuania, Estonia, Finland, Spain, Portugal, Balkans.

and to 230 million in 1981. Migration of different sorts and at different intensities has continued right up to the present, and the United States, and especially its cities, are made up of an immense complexity of ethnic groups.

Several distinct stages may be recognised in this process. First, the 'old' migration began in the earlier and middle nineteenth century. It consisted mainly of groups from north-west Europe, principally Great Britain and Ireland, but increasingly from Germany and Scandinavia. Chain migration, where information was passed from one family in America back to another in the village of origin, often played a vital role, for example in the establishment of Swedish migrants in Minnesota. By 1900 something like half of the immigrants into the United States went on prepaid tickets with their fares paid by relatives already in America. Several groups, particularly the Irish, began to play a distinctive and lasting role in American society. Most migration was permanent, cost and time acting to discourage temporary movement. German emigration began in the second decade of the nineteenth century, after the end of the Napoleonic wars and soon became a complex and varied flow whose volume reacted to political and economic fluctuations. Tracing the route that migrants took is often instructive: some sailed from the Dutch ports and others from Hamburg or Bremen. Cargo such as tobacco came in one direction over the Atlantic and migrants returned in the other. Hamburg's bulk trade was with England and so the migrants went from there to Hull, then overland by canal barge, and set sail from Liverpool.

Migration from the 'old' sources peaked by the 1880s and was gradually replaced by the 'new' migration (see Table 3.4) from southern and eastern Europe. Italians, Russians, Slovaks, Poles, Croatians, Romanians and Greeks flooded in. Jews arrived from many countries and the general pattern of Jewish immigration is shown in Fig. 3.4. In the Civil War decade, the percentage of immigration from northern and western Europe was 89%; by the decade 1901-10, it had fallen to 22%. Much of the immigration was via Ellis Island in New York. Although a large number of these 'new' immigrants did settle permanently, it has recently been suggested that more were temporary than amongst the 'old' migrants. This may have been due to the nature of the migrants themselves, but also to the nature of demand: for example, the demand for a mobile, unskilled labour force for building railways and canals, rather than a family-based movement of settlers. Some of the 'new' migration took on an almost seasonal character, therefore, with the migrants intending to make their fortune and return home. There were important peaks of migration in the 1880s and especially in the years before the First World War. As Table 3.4 shows, the 'new' migration

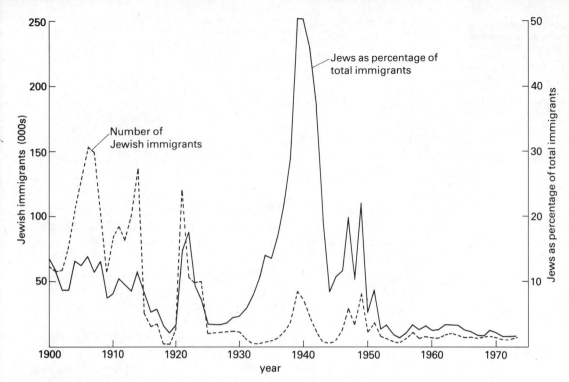

Fig 3.4 Jewish immigration to the USA, 1900-73, showing the total numbers of Jewish immigrants and their proportion of all immigrants. The largest inflows came in the years before, and immediately after, the First World War, although Jews formed a relatively small proportion of the very large total influx. By contrast, with the general slow-down of immigration, the Jewish inflow from 1930 to 1950, and in particular during 1939-42 accounted for up to half of all immigration. *Source:* data from Dinnerstein and Reimers (1977), pp. 172-3.

from Europe reached a peak of well over one million per annum for the period 1906–10. Many of these were bound for the USA so that (Table 3.5) immigration accounted for over 40% of population growth in the peak years.

The Italians are a particularly interesting case of emigration, for they occur still in our next example of contemporary migrants. They were one of the most important groups in this 'new' migration to the USA and are a good example of the way in which we must look at the conditions in the country of origin as much as, or more than, at the pull of the USA itself. In the 1880s, for example, the fall of cereal and other agricultural prices, which brought a crisis to farmers all over Europe, came upon Italy just as the population was growing quickly. In addition the peasantry, in the south especially, lived in acute poverty: soil erosion, malaria, extreme fragmentation of holdings, high taxes and a lack of governmental concern made emigration an obvious release. The hilly districts, poorest and most populous, provided the first migrants; then the pull of emigration spread slowly to the coastal regions and after 1900 came a great outpouring from Sicily. The bulk of the Italians in the 'new' migration to the USA came from the south, forming easy prey for the 'padroni' in the eastern cities of the states who hired out workers in huge bands and charged them large

Table 3.5 Immigration to the USA. *Source:* Thomas (1973), 131.

Decade	Rate of increase in foreign-born population (%)	Immigration as % of population growth
1870–80	20	29
1880–90	39	43
1890–1900	12	32
1900–10	31	42
1910–20	3	17
1920–30	3	22

Table 3.6 Population of Italian origin living in the USA. *Source:* Piore (1979), 155.

Year	Born in Italy (000s)	Born in US of Italian or mixed parentage (000s)	Born abroad (%)
1900	484	255	65.4
1910	1,343	722	63.5
1920	1,610	1,751	47.9
1930	1,790	2,756	39.4
1940	1,624	2,971	35.3
1950	1,427	3,143	31.2

commissions. The number of permanent migrants of Italian origin—both born in Italy and of Italian parentage—thus increased rapidly and became a part of the American scene. As Table 3.6 shows, the Italian influence—reaching over 3 million by the 1950s—was maintained despite the fact that the proportion actually born abroad had declined progressively. Strong links were developed both with villages and towns of origin in Italy and within the Italian communities themselves—as the film *The Godfather*, for example, so potently illustrated!

Despite a certain degree of continuity in some flows, such as the Italians, the First World War marked a major turning-point in immigration. The War itself interrupted flows, but of principal importance was the legislation of 1923 which imposed a strict quota system, giving priority to relatives of earlier migrants. This led to both a decline in overall numbers of immigrants and a shift from temporary to permanent settlement: the proportion of foreign-born in the United States who had been there for ten years or less declined from 45% in 1880-90 to 19% by 1920-30 and 1% by 1930-40. A second-generation labour force emerged, which gradually made its way up the social ladder.

One product of this stabilisation in numbers and upward social mobility was to create a vacuum at the bottom of the labour market. A third stage in the migration process does not properly concern us here, as it was mainly a matter of internal migration, but is a good illustration of the similarities between international and internal movements in terms of cause and, to an extent, effect. From around 1915 onwards a massive movement of black workers from the rural south to the industrial cities of the north began. This slackened a little in the 1930s but continued apace in the 1940s and 1950s, the blacks quickly coming to occupy a distinctive place in both the labour market and the social geography of the American city.

A new stage in the migration process in the USA that we may recognise has arisen from the 1950s and 1960s and again takes on the form of international movement, mainly clandestine migration from Latin America and the Caribbean. It includes large groups from Mexico, the Dominican Republic and Haiti. Mexican migration, whose distribution is shown in Fig. 3.5, can be traced back in fact to rather earlier periods and is distinctive partly because the majority go into agriculture and partly because there have been occasional periods of forced repatriation. Public antipathy towards illegal migration has increased in the USA, as it has in western Europe, in response to rising unemployment from the mid-1970s. There was some migration from the English-speaking Caribbean after the Second World War, but large-scale movement from Spanish-speaking areas is a product of the 1960s. Puerto Rican migration is an interesting case: large numbers went to New York in the 1940s and 1950s and the present community there shares many of the problems of unemployment

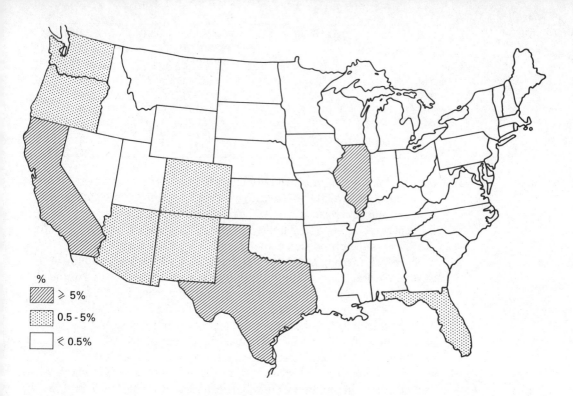

%
|/// | ≥ 5%
|:::| 0.5 - 5%
| | ≤ 0.5%

Fig 3.5 Estimated percentages, by destination, of undocumented migrants from Mexico to the USA, 1978/79. The pattern is of very concentrated destinations: over 50% go to California and almost one-quarter to Texas. Only 9 states attract more than 0.5% of the total Mexican immigrants. They clearly favour neighbouring, western states, with the exception of Florida and Illinois, where high wages have proved attractive. *Source:* R.C. Jones (1982), 'Channelization of undocumented Mexican migrants to the US'. *Economic Geography* 58,2:168.

and welfare of the black population. Elsewhere, until the 1960s, Puerto Ricans were employed in agriculture and since then there has been increased penetration into industry and urban areas. There has been a considerable increase in immigration to the USA, both legal and illegal and including refugees, since the mid-1970s which has given rise to concern. Legal permanent admissions to the USA rose from 450,000 in 1976 to 800,000 in 1980, compared with a figure of under 300,000 as recently as 1965. In addition, estimates of the annual inflow of illegal migrants are as high as 500,000. The United States remains the major country of destination in the world for international migrants. There have been pressures for tighter control: the Immigration Reform and Control Act proposed in 1982 would increase border checks, set new annual ceilings for total immigration (425,000 immigrants) and for individual countries (20,000 annually per country, except for Mexico and Canada which could send twice that number) and allow some legalisation of status for illegal aliens already resident.

This example serves to show, then, the way in which a complex interplay of forces at origin and destination shapes migration flows and how successive waves of migrants have come in at the bottom of the labour market, replacing earlier generations. In the twentieth century, and not least today, international movement has posed fundamental questions of political control and policy which may be seen in the broader context discussed in Chapter 6. Certainly, the result of migration is everywhere visible on the face of American society.

Migration in western Europe since 1945

Experience of international migration in Europe since 1945 has come as a sharp contradiction to the emigration that characterised the continent in the nineteenth and early twentieth centuries. This chapter has already

North Africans form an important part of France's immigrant population. In 1981 there were some 817,000 Algerians, 445,000 Moroccans and 193,000 Tunisians. Together they accounted for just over one-third of France's total foreign population.

hinted at the existence of a large immigrant population in many countries of north-west Europe, the product of waves of immigration during the later 1950s and 1960s. For the continent has been increasingly divided into those countries sending and those countries receiving migrants. Into the latter category come the UK, France, West Germany and the smaller states of Switzerland, Sweden, the Netherlands and Belgium: some 15 million migrants and their families have had a significant impact on national and regional rates of population growth and on cultural and social evolution, especially in the cities. The main 'exporting' countries were Italy, Spain, Portugal, Yugoslavia and Greece, countries on the southern fringe with lower levels of development and surplus agricultural populations.

The mix of nationalities in the receiving countries varies a great deal, as many have recruited from outside Europe too, partly in relation to colonial links established in the last century. France, for example, draws many migrants from North Africa, while in contrast Germany's major foreign groups are from Turkey, Greece, Yugoslavia, Italy and Spain. The distribution of the main nationalities by countries in 1974—the year at which immigration reached a peak—is shown in Fig. 3.6, and the overall importance of foreigners in the total population in 1980 in Table 3.7. The United Kingdom is a notable exception in two respects: first that, unlike many other countries, settlement of migrants soon became predominantly family-based and permanent in intent; secondly, that the balance of nationalities was very different, the main groups being, after the Irish, West Indian, Indian and Pakistani. The Benelux countries are also distinctive: the Netherlands, for example, had a large inflow of Indonesians in the 1950s, followed by the Surinamese in the early 1970s. Different nationalities play different roles in population growth and structure and pose different problems of integration and assimilation. Age structures (Fig. 3.7) are an illustration: the age/sex pyramid for foreigners in France is severely distorted towards males in the age-group 20–40 for the Algerians or black Africans, whereas the pyramid is more

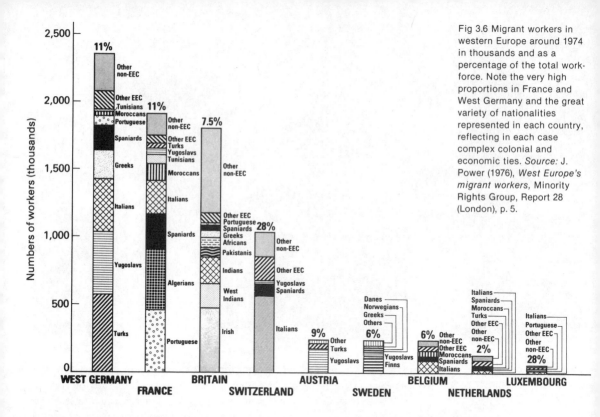

Fig 3.6 Migrant workers in western Europe around 1974 in thousands and as a percentage of the total work-force. Note the very high proportions in France and West Germany and the great variety of nationalities represented in each country, reflecting in each case complex colonial and economic ties. *Source:* J. Power (1976), *West Europe's migrant workers*, Minority Rights Group, Report 28 (London), p. 5.

Table 3.7 Total foreign resident population in the principal immigration countries, Western Europe, 1980. *Source:* A. Golini (1982), *Size and growth of immigrant populations* (Council of Europe, Strasbourg), 12.

	000s	% of total population
Belgium	903	9.2
France	4,148	7.7
Germany	4,453	7.2
Netherlands	477	3.4
Sweden	422	5.1
Switzerland	893	14.2

balanced for Spanish or Italians who have a much longer history of migration. Disparities in demographic and social structure are heightened by the concentration of immigrants in cities and industrial areas: in Britain (see Chapter 5), in London, the West Midlands and Yorkshire and, in France, in Paris, Lyons and Marseilles. Fig. 3.8 shows the age pyramid for Munich in 1980 and the contribution made by foreigners, particularly in the age groups 20–45.

Of the many aspects of immigration that may be taken up, one is of particular interest: the adaptation of migrant flows to economic recession in the 1970s. Table 3.8 shows clearly that there have been three phases in immigration over the last decade in the EEC of the Nine. Net migration was maintained at over 500,000 per annum up to the oil crisis year of 1973, after which the ensuing recession led to a stabilisation of flows and even a net outflow during 1975. In the later 1970s net immigration resumed but was made up largely of family movements, wives and children joining already resident male workers. This trend is well reflected in the experience of individual states, both traditional 'sending' and 'receiving' countries. West Germany swung sharply from being a large net importer of labour up to 1973 to experiencing net emigration during 1974, 1975 and 1976. Latterly, family movements have created a new, though

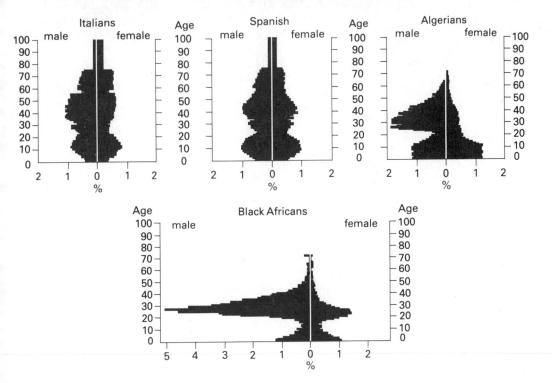

Fig 3.7 Age and sex
structures for immigrant
groups in France 1975. Those
groups with a longer history
of immigration, for example,
Italians or Spanish show a
more balanced age and sex
structure; whereas more
recent immigrants like the
Algerians or Black Africans
tend to be dominated by
males of active working age.
Source: based on M. Tribalat-
Brahimi (1981), 'Chronique de
l'immigration', *Population*
36,1:154–5.

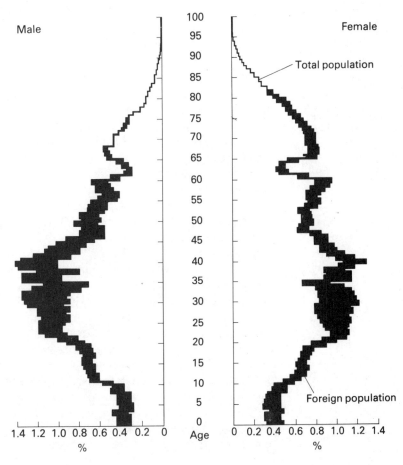

Fig 3.8 Age and sex structure
of Munich's population in
1980, showing the proportion
of foreigners in each age-
group. Particularly marked is
the contribution to the male
age-groups 20–45. Note also
the extreme narrowing of the
base of the pyramid as a
result of sharply declining
birth rates since the
mid-1960s. *Source:* Alliance
nationale contre la
dépopulation (1980), *Chute de
la natalité: une menace pour
la prospérité* (Paris), p. 26.

Table 3.8 Net migration rates for some major EEC countries in the 1970s (in 000s). *Source:* Eurostat: *Demographic statistics 1980* (Luxembourg, 1982).

	EEC of the Nine	West Germany	France	Belgium	Italy	(Greece)
1970	663	560	180	4	− 47	− 46
1971	554	454	143	24	− 49	− 15
1972	574	336	102	14	91	− 1
1973	696	387	106	19	191	− 43
1974	124	− 9	30	25	111	− 19
1975	− 40	− 199	25	25	82	59
1976	5	− 73	0	8	58	56
1977	96	34	0	5	67	22
1978	215	115	0	− 3	48	36
1979	325	246	0	2	29	12
1980	329	312	0	− 2	49	89

Fig 3.9 Components of population change in West Germany 1960–80. A declining birth rate has produced natural decrease (more deaths than births) since the early 1970s. Net migration has fluctuated more markedly. Apart from 1967, Germany was a net importer of labour up to 1974, when recession slowed down the inflows. Recently, family movements have again made the net migration balance positive. *Source of data:* Eurostat (1982), *Demographic statistics 1980* (Luxembourg).

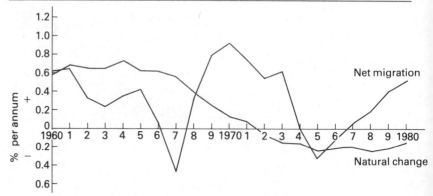

smaller, net immigration (Fig. 3.9). France went through a similar transition in the early years of the decade, although the severity with which immigration restrictions have been imposed since 1974 means that net migration has remained at zero in every year from 1976 onwards. The experience of two main sending countries—Italy and Greece—is to some extent a mirror image of these trends. Italy remained a net exporter during 1970 and 1971 and Greece up to 1974, then both became net importers, especially during the mid-1970s, as workers began to return home. While both remained net importers of migrants up to the end of the decade, the easing of return flows and the more liberal policies towards family movements in some 'receiving' countries meant that net migration rates declined again.

Thus, experience in western Europe over the last decade illustrates the sensitivity of international migration to the joint pressures of economic recession and governmental controls. In all the countries of mass immigration during the 1960s, immigration policy both with respect to numbers of arrivals and to coping with a large, ethnically diverse population has proved a lively political issue. There is no doubt that whatever may have been the original intentions of the countries or the migrants concerned, many of those moving from the underdeveloped European periphery and beyond have become permanent residents in the north-west European countries. Equally, for the traditional southern European 'exporters', the drying up of one of their sources of external revenue and the problems posed by migrants returning home are a feature of the 1980s. One interesting further development since the mid-1970s, a result of the same trend in the world economy, is that large numbers of workers have gone to the oil-exporting countries of the Middle East: about three million at present, two-thirds of them from the region itself and the rest from south and south-east Asia.

4 Migration and urban growth

Introduction

The increasing concentration of population in urban areas has become a feature of most countries in both the developed and developing worlds. The urban expansion which characterised the countries of western Europe in the nineteenth century has been duplicated and magnified during the twentieth in many parts of Africa, Latin America and Asia. Although much urban growth is a result of natural increase, much also may be explained by migration, transferring people from the rural to the urban environment. Urbanisation both reflects migration and itself stimulates new forms of mobility: indeed, today, in many societies rural−urban movement has all but played itself out. In some countries, like the USA or parts of Europe, traditional flows of migration have been reversed so that large urban areas are now losing population. In this chapter we look at some of the forces underlying movement and then take examples from Britain, western Europe and the developing world.

'Push' and 'pull' factors

The process of urban growth, and the patterns of migration associated with it, reflect underlying economic change of revolutionary proportions. Migration reflects the social imbalance often created by rapid economic change and may represent a mechanism of adjustment to it. Internal migration has many resemblances in cause and effect to the international flows discussed in the previous chapter, although the dramatic aspects of forced movement and the marked cultural differences produced are

Irish immigrants in Circus Street, Liverpool in 1895. In the later nineteenth century, the Irish were one of the most mobile populations in the world. Many came to English cities like Liverpool where they formed a distinctive element in the growing industrial working class.

generally lacking. At the most general level, we may see the pattern of rural—urban movement as part of the general process of 'modernisation' central to the idea of the mobility transition discussed in Chapter 2. Thus, we may think of states as being at various points in the transition from rural to urban, the movement from countryside to town which characterised Europe of the nineteenth century still being in full flood in parts of the developing world today, although under very different conditions.

At the level of specific cases, it may be useful to think in terms of a systems approach: the case outlined earlier was drawn from an example of rural—urban migration in Africa. Economic development breaks down the self-sufficiency of a local agricultural economy and migrants become part of a system of close links between village and town. Many of the economic and social influences, and matters of individual behaviour, outlined in Chapter 2 are clearly relevant here and it is usual to think of these in terms of 'push' and 'pull' factors. 'Push' factors, encouraging people to leave the land, include overpopulation or the distress resulting from an imbalance between resources and population numbers; poverty and low wages; poor climate and physical environment; agricultural decline, including declining markets for particular types of produce; the break-up of traditional communities and social ties as urban influences make themselves felt; the lack of social services, including education and housing. 'Pull' factors include opportunities to earn better wages in the town; a wider range of occupational possibilities; better provision for housing, education and other community facilities; and the lure of new activities, environment or people such as the cultural, intellectual and recreational activities of a large metropolis. In terms of 'pull' factors much depends on an individual's perception of them, as his information about new locations will be less accurate than his immediate experience of factors 'pushing' him to move.

The move from countryside to town is of overwhelming importance in understanding the current geographical pattern of population distribution in most states, as the following examples show, yet we should not forget that in developed states recent trends in internal migration have favoured movement between and within cities and in some cases away from the great metropolitan centres. The United States, for example, passed through the great phase of expansion of huge cities, aided by immigration and movement from the countryside, but during the 1970s experienced new trends. Each year between 1970 and 1975, for every 100 people who moved to the large cities, 131 moved out. Movement out of large cities is not simply a 'spillover' of people into suburban areas but a real movement further afield, to smaller places. Whereas only one of America's twenty-five largest urban centres (Pittsburgh) lost population during the 1960s, nine were declining by the late 1970s: New York, Los Angeles, Philadelphia, St Louis, Pittsburgh, Newark, Cleveland, Seattle and Cincinnati. A similar phenomenon is noted for Europe below, but let us first of all turn our attention to the way in which urban growth was generated by movement from countryside to town.

Migration and urban growth in the industrial revolution in Britain

In the economies of Britain and western Europe, the industrial revolution of the eighteenth and nineteenth centuries saw a definitive shift from an agricultural to a manufacturing economy. In Britain, for example, from the middle of the eighteenth century, regional shifts in population growth were a more and more complex balance between natural change (an increasing dominance of births over deaths) and net migration. Many works have shown that even before the industrial revolution, a picture of immobility is inappropriate and there was often a steady drift to the towns. The population of Tudor and Stuart England, for example, was highly mobile. The population of London grew from about 50,000 to 60,000 in the 1520s to 575,000 by 1700: high mortality indicates that immigration must have played a dominant role. It has been estimated that perhaps 8,000 more people moved to London every year than left it in the period 1650–1700. Some migrants were already moving over considerable distances: an analysis of working men living in Stepney and Whitechapel between 1580 and 1639 showed that well over two-thirds came from more than fifty miles away. For provincial towns, migrants were also a necessary element for growth, but they came from generally shorter distances.

Despite these observations, there is nevertheless no doubt that the towns which began to mushroom in Britain from the mid-eighteenth century were of a different order of magnitude and influence. A new kind of city emerged during the nineteenth century: as A.F. Weber in his classic *The growth of cities in the nineteenth century* (1899) observed: 'The most remarkable social phenomenon of the present century is the concentration of population in cities... The tendency towards concentration or agglomeration is all but universal in the western world.' Increased division of labour, increased specialisation, larger production units, more complex market mechanisms promoted this process and assured a shift in the occupational structure of economies. New institutions associated with advancing capitalist systems replaced or remodelled the old. The pace of change and its inception varied greatly within western Europe. Britain was the clear leader in the field, followed rather later by Germany or France and later still by, for example, the countries of southern Europe. Yet the process was inexorable: while it took many decades for other countries to equal Britain's rate of urban growth, nevertheless from the mid-nineteenth century the continental peasantry was beginning to be uprooted. Urbanisation was also a symptom of the growth of the international economy and of interdependence. The pattern of international migration between countries and continents was an aspect of this process, of which internal movement is to some degree a natural extension.

Certainly migration to the city became a dominant theme in the evolution of social structures in the nineteenth century. Thomas Hardy well summarised the process he saw going on all around in his fictional Wessex:

'These families, who had formed the backbone of the village life in the past, who were the depositaries of the village traditions, had to seek refuge in the large centres; the process, humorously designated by statisticians as "the tendency of the rural population towards the large towns", being really the tendency of water to flow uphill when forced by machinery.' (*Tess of the d'Urbervilles: A pure woman,* first edition 1891, New Wessex Edition 1974, Macmillan, p. 401.)

Movements had, indeed, profound effects on areas of origin and destination. In the former, migration may at first have allowed an excess of population to be skimmed off but later led to the enfeeblement of much of the countryside. In the latter, the arrival of migrants in large numbers transformed urban growth rates, demographic structures and the internal social structure of the city. The development of much social thought and theory dates from this period of transformation; the debate, for example, over the relative rise or fall of living standards and the fate of the poor. It was no mere coincidence that Karl Marx was writing at a time of unparalleled urban change nor indeed, at a different level, that Ravenstein was formulating his general principles of migration in the later nineteenth century. There was an increasing tendency to see social evolution in terms of polarity between a traditional or pre-industrial society and a modern or urban-industrial society, although it was certainly not the case that social theorists agreed that this transformation was always a beneficial one.

Table 4.1 Urban and rural populations in England and Wales, 1801–1911. *Source:* adapted from Lawton (1978), 342.

	Total		Rural*		Urban		% of total in towns of	
	(millions)	(% change)	(millions)	(% of total)	(millions)	(% of total)	< 10,000	> 100,000
1801	8.9	—	5.9	66.2	3.0	33.8	9.9	11.0
1811	10.2	14.0	6.4	63.4	3.7	36.6	10.8	13.7
1821	12.0	18.1	7.2	60.0	4.8	40.0	11.0	15.6
1831	13.9	15.8	7.7	55.7	6.2	44.3	10.6	18.6
1841	15.9	14.3	8.2	51.7	7.7	48.3	10.0	20.7
1851	17.9	12.6	8.2	46.0	9.7	54.0	9.9	24.8
1861	20.1	11.9	8.3	41.3	11.8	58.7	9.8	28.8
1871	22.7	13.2	7.9	34.8	14.8	65.2	10.8	32.6
1881	25.9	14.7	7.8	30.0	18.2	70.0	10.5	36.2
1891	29.0	11.6	7.4	25.5	21.6	74.5	10.2	39.4
1901	32.5	12.2	7.2	22.0	25.4	78.0	8.9	43.6
1911	36.1	10.9	7.6	21.1	28.5	78.9	8.8	43.8

*Not confined solely to agricultural rural areas. For estimates of the truly rural see Lawton (1978), 342.

Britain represents the example *par excellence* of the processes of social change which accompanied urbanisation. Data on urban growth are given in Table 4.1 for the nineteenth century. A remarkable picture emerges: the total population of England and Wales increased from just under 9 million to over 36 million between 1801 and 1911. The urban population rose to a total of 28.5 million in 1911 compared with a mere 3 million in 1801, representing 78.9 and 33.8% of the total in respective years. The rural population thus grew slightly until mid-century and fell slowly thereafter, although its share in the total fell continuously throughout the century. There was also a marked change in the nature of the towns themselves: the proportion of the total population living in towns of more than 100,000 rose dramatically from 11% to more than 40% during the century.

The contribution of migration to the considerable regional shifts in population which underlay this national pattern is more complex than might at first appear. The balance of migration and natural increase

Fig 4.1 Population trends in England and Wales 1851–1911, showing the relative balance of net migration and natural increase in determining population growth or decline. Net in-migration is particularly strong in urban areas and net out-migration in rural areas, producing an increasing disparity between population gain and loss.
Source: Lawton (1978), p. 344.

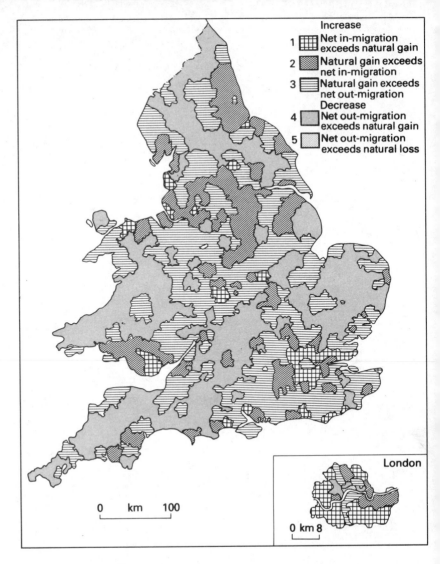

Increase
1 Net in-migration exceeds natural gain
2 Natural gain exceeds net in-migration
3 Natural gain exceeds net out-migration

Decrease
4 Net out-migration exceeds natural gain
5 Net out-migration exceeds natural loss

London

0   km   100

0 km 8

varies both geographically and over time. During the period 1780–1831, there was a national population increase of some 83%, and an increasing level of urbanisation saw considerable in-migration to London and the big provincial cities. In London and the metropolitan counties, of an overall increase of about 1,364,000, three-quarters of a million was contributed by net migration, although in some northern industrial regions of England growth depended largely on their own natural increase. For later decades, the calculation of components of change becomes rather more reliable as more data became available. Fig. 4.1 and Table 4.2 show for the period 1841–1911 how this balance worked out on the ground. Fig. 4.1 draws attention to the polarisation of population in a relatively few areas. The chequered map areas are those where net immigration exceeds natural gain and they are confined to restricted urban areas in most of the main economic growth areas: South Wales, London, parts of the Midlands, the North West and the North East. The second category is also of interest for our argument, since it indicates that there were large areas within industrialising regions where natural increase remained much more important than migration in maintaining growth. In a general sense, through the categories 4 and 5, the map shows the increasing national

Table 4.2 The growth of
population in England and
Wales, 1841–1911. *Source:*
adapted from Lawton (1978),
332–3.

	Natural increase 1841–1911	Net gain (+) or loss (−) by migration 1841–1911	Ratio of migrational gain or loss to natural increase (%)	Total percentage increase 1841–1911
1. Towns				
(a) Large				
London	3,802,252	+ 1,250,511	+ 32.9	223.7
8 northern	2,747,306	+ 893,337	+ 32.5	234.7
(b) Textile				
22 northern	1,705,779	+ 89,933	+ 5.3	129.5
(c) Industrial				
14 northern	1,361,999	− 152,994	− 11.2	200.4
11 southern	428,363	− 15,679	− 3.7	139.4
(d) Old				
7 northern	343,006	+ 15,944	+ 4.6	123.9
13 southern	732,973	− 22,004	− 3.0	107.0
(e) Residential				
9 northern	211,895	+ 140,230	+ 66.2	170.2
26 southern	750,483	+ 327,362	+ 43.6	155.7
(f) Military				
16 southern	616,644	+ 124,948	+ 20.3	157.5
Northern towns	6,369,985	+ 986,450	+ 15.5	188.2
Southern towns	6,331,165	+ 1,665,138	+ 26.3	182.3
All towns	12,701,150	+ 2,651,588	+ 20.9	174.3
2. Colliery districts				
9 northern	3,363,112	+ 650,548	+ 19.3	304.0
3. Rural residues:				
12 northern	2,093,257	− 1,643,770	− 78.6	18.5
12 southern	3,208,729	− 2,863,266	− 89.2	9.2
Total rural residues	5,301,986	− 4,507,036	− 85.0	12.9

division between areas of growth and areas of decline, the natural increases of the countryside being skimmed off by migration to the cities after mid-century.

Table 4.2 puts flesh on the bones of this regional argument by comparing natural increase and migration for different types of region. As the century progressed, it is probably true to say, migration fluctuations became relatively more important than changes in birth and death in determining regional redistribution, although we should underestimate neither the enduring regional variability of the latter nor its temporal variations. In the rural areas, as Table 4.2 shows, net migration removed some 4.5 million people from the countryside, absorbing 85% of the natural increase. Although birth rates in rural areas remained relatively high well into the nineteenth century, continuous out-migration eventually had its effect and there was a sharp downturn in natural increase after 1891. Richard Lawton's analysis of the contribution of migration has shown that net movement accounted for over one-sixth of urban population increase between 1841 and 1911: in London migration contributed one-quarter of the total increase. He also shows, though, that in northern industrial areas variations in the economic climate meant that not every area gained by migration in each decade. The calculations in Table 4.2 show the degree of variation by area. The contribution of

Table 4.3 Decline in the agricultural labour force in Sweden and the USA, 1920–70. *Source:* Kingsley Davis 'The effect of outmigration on regions of origin', Ch. 10 in A. A. Brown and E. Neuberger (eds.), (1977) 152.

	Sweden		USA	
	no. (000s)	change per decade (%)	no. (000s)	change per decade (%)
1920	724.7	—	11,449	—
1930	707.6	− 2.4	10,472	− 8.5
1940	687.7*	− 1.9	9,140	− 12.7
1950	578.7	− 29.2	7,160	− 21.7
1960	408.1	− 29.5	5,458	− 23.8
1970	315.0*	− 40.4	3,462	− 36.6

*Relates to 1935, 1965 with rate calculated on decadal basis.

migration in London and the larger towns was considerable: in the eight large northern cities, there was a migration gain of just under a million. Migration was also very important for the residential towns and some colliery districts, although in the industrial towns there was an overall loss, especially after 1881 as their economic fortunes declined. Certainly, in individual decades migration responded directly to spurts of economic growth, for example in 1861–70, 1871–80 and 1890–1901.

It is also worth noting at this point that figures such as those given in Table 4.2 conceal as much as they reveal in the sense that a net migration figure is both highly approximate and is made up of a huge number of individual moves and individual decisions. One way of looking at the total impact of migration over a number of years is to use information on place of birth. Thus, by 1911, in much of south-east England over 40% of the population was born outside the area and in most towns in the Greater London area this figure was over 50%. We shall look at the detailed effects on city life in the next chapter, but the general effect of these processes of intense migration in nineteenth-century Britain was to produce a weakened rural social structure and crowded, quickly growing, more accessible cities where new social conditions, new attitudes and new communities grew up.

In estimating the effect of migration we need to remember that it was strongly selective by age and sex: the countryside lost many more younger migrants than old. A further important point is that as urbanisation proceeded in Britain, migration itself became more complex: by the beginning of the present century, movement between cities and within cities had begun to overtake rural–urban movement in volume and effect.

A European comparison

The British case is important not only in its own right but because it set the pattern for European, and other rapidly evolving, economies in the nineteenth and twentieth centuries. Economic development, industrialisation and urbanisation have gradually fostered the demise of the rural peasant economy. The seeds of this change were certainly sown in the nineteenth century but it was in many cases not until the twentieth that it had its full effect. Thus, in Table 4.3 we see for Sweden and the USA the dramatic fall in the agricultural labour force over the last fifty years, the rate of decline accelerating in the decades since the Second World War. In the USA, the agricultural labour force fell by almost 8

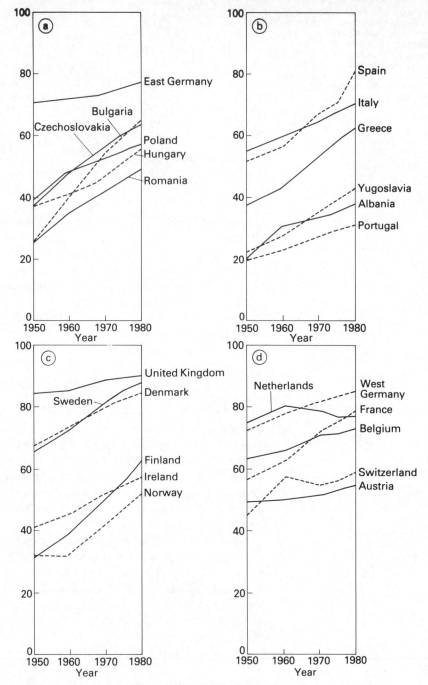

Fig 4.2 Percentage of population living in cities in (a) Eastern Europe (b) Southern Europe (c) Northern Europe (d) Western Europe 1950–80. The general trend has been consistently upwards in all regions, although with some slowing of urban growth in parts of Northern and Western Europe during the 1970s (see Fig 4.3). *Source:* J. Bourgeois-Pichat (1981), 'Recent demographic change in western Europe: an assessment, *Population and Development Review* 7,1:34.

million in fifty years. The overall proportions in the primary sector for European countries emphasise again the recency of the change. In West Germany and Belgium, the proportion fell by two-thirds, in Italy by more than a half between 1950 and 1972. Few countries had reached a level as low as that of the UK, of 2.7% in 1972, although most were tending strongly in that direction. In terms of the proportion of population living in cities in major European states, the total between 1950 and 1980 has been consistently upwards (Fig. 4.2). Most states have well over 50% of their population in towns (Table 4.4) and many have a much higher proportion (84.7% for West Germany in 1980, for example). Very recent

Tale 4.4 Percentage of population urban (national definitions) in selected European countries, 1970 and estimates for 1980 and 2000. *Source:* J. Bourgeois-Pichat (1981) 'Recent demographic change in Western Europe: an assessment', *Population and Development Review 7*, 1:33.

	1970	1980	2000
United Kingdom	88.5	90.8	93.7
France	71.7	78.0	85.4
West Germany	81.3	84.7	89.4
Italy	64.5	69.3	78.1
Sweden	81.1	87.2	92.3

Fig 4.3 Annual net migration, in thousands, into metropolitan regions of Japan and selected European countries 1945 to late 1970s. All cases show high rates of immigration during the 1950s and 1960s and a drastic reduction during the 1970s, indicating urban deconcentration. *Source:* Jones (1981), p. 235, after D.R. Vining and T. Kontuly (1978), 'Population dispersal from major metropolitan regions: an international comparison', *International Regional Science Review* 3,1:49–73.

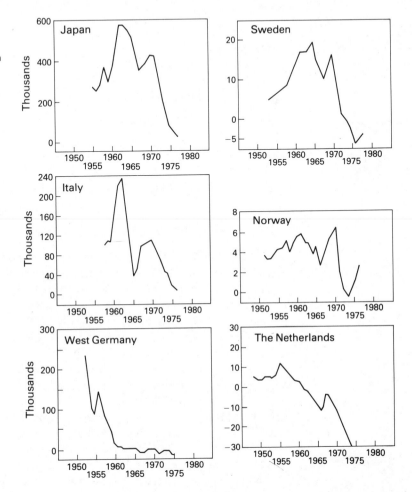

trends, though, show that the simple movement from countryside to town had played itself out in many developed countries by the early 1970s. Fig. 4.3 shows how the rate of net migration into major urban areas in six countries has slowed down sharply during the 1970s, indicating a deconcentration of population from many metropolitan regions both into immediate hinterlands and into more peripheral regions. Results of the 1981 census for England and Wales (see Table 1.2) confirm that this is the case: London and major urban areas showed considerable population declines over the decade 1971–81.

France is an excellent case of a country where the transition from a rural, agricultural to an urban, industrial society was achieved both later and more quickly than in the UK. France had more than one quarter of its labour force in the primary sector in 1950 and this was more than halved over the following two decades. Although the speed and recency of change are remarkable, these trends may nevertheless be traced back to

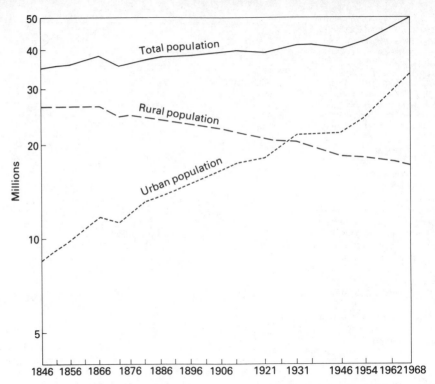

Fig 4.4a Population change in France 1846–1968 (logarithmic scale), showing that in a steadily rising national population, urban dwellers account for a progressively greater proportion.

the nineteenth century. The maximum rural population was achieved in many rural areas by the 1850s since when there has been fairly continuous rural migration to the cities. Some areas were much slower to follow this lead. Brittany, for example, did not peak until the early part of the present century. The accumulated effect by 1975 was considerable: many areas especially in the mountainous Central Massif, Alps or Pyrenees had lost more than 50% of their population since the maximum. Between 1851 and 1968 the proportion of the French population living in the countryside declined from 74% to 34% so that, despite a rising national population, there were about 12 million fewer rural dwellers. This process was much less marked in France than in England and Wales by 1900, but it is true nevertheless that there was no region, and scarcely a village, that by the First World War had not sent some of its inhabitants to the cities. The Paris region grew more than threefold (6 million people) from the mid-nineteenth to the mid-twentieth century and provided a focus for migrants. The capital gradually strengthened its administrative, economic and cultural grip on the provinces. Equally, urban centres outside Paris—Lyons, Marseilles, Bordeaux and so forth—came increasingly to exercise influence over their rural hinterlands and to aid the process of integration of peasant society into urban life. The general evolution of urban versus rural population is given in Fig. 4.4a and of individual cities in Fig. 4.4b, c.

The contrast between rural decline and urban growth which migration produced has been illustrated in several ways. For example, by the 1930s only 16 out of 90 *départements* had larger total populations than ever before. Gravier, in his famous study of Paris and the 'French desert', showed that between 1851 and 1931 overall population increase meant population decline for 95% of the national territory. Another author, Eugen Weber, has likened the general process to colonisation: 'we are talking about the process of acculturation: the civilisation of the French

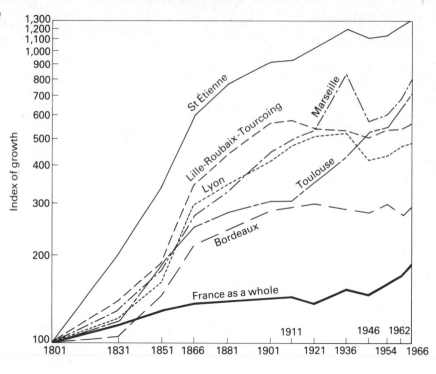

Fig 4.4b Population growth of selected French cities since 1801. The index plots relative growth from a common starting-point of 100 in 1801. Note the rapid urban expansion from the middle of the nineteenth century, particularly in the strongly industrialising areas of St Etienne, and Lille-Roubaix-Tourcoing.

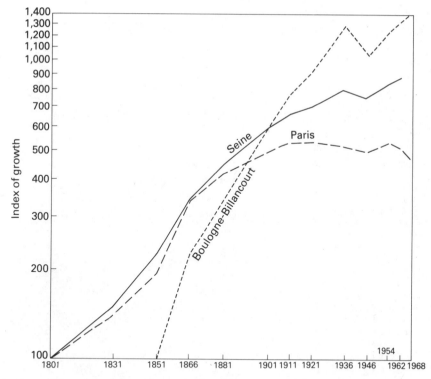

Fig 4.4c Population growth in the Paris conurbation since 1801 (and 1851). The city of Paris itself grew rapidly during the nineteenth century and then stabilised, to the benefit of the wider Seine district and of individual suburban areas like Boulogne-Billancourt. *Sources for 4.4 a–c:* G. Dupeux (1972), *French society, 1789–1970* (Methuen, London), pp. 11, 14, 15.

by urban France, the disintegration of local cultures by modernity and their absorption into the dominant civilisation of Paris and the schools... the... rural masses had to be integrated into the dominant culture as they had been integrated into an administrative entity'. Migration played a key part in this process of establishing links between rural and urban, stimulating the flow of new ideas, rising expectations, different political outlooks. The accumulating effects of migration meant that more and

61

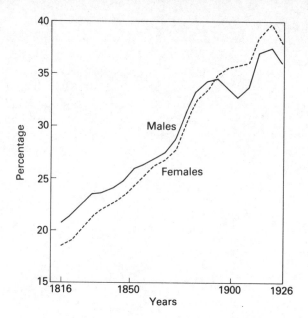

Fig 4.5 Percentage of the French population aged 45 living outside their *département* of birth for generations born 1816–1926. Increasing migration uproots more and more people from their native towns and villages. For the generations born in the 1920s, more than 35% live outside their areas of birth. *Source:* Y. Tugault (1973), *La Mesure de la mobilité. Cinq études sur les migrations internes.* Cahier de l'INED, No. 67 (PUF, Paris), p. 36.

more people were living outside their areas of birth: Fig. 4.5 shows how rapidly these proportions grew for both men and women, to exceed 35% for the 1920s generations. The result of this was both to weaken peasant society and to create new urban communities. The mark of migration is everywhere apparent in the modern French city. In Paris, for example, the mushrooming of new suburbs between the Wars, and especially since the 1950s, was in response to the floods of migrants from the countryside. Compared with inhabitants of large British cities, the French city-dweller of the 1980s still has strong rural roots. The French adaptation to urban living seems thus much more uneasy and unstable than the British.

Indeed, there is some evidence in very recent trends that France is

Fig 4.6 Population trends in (a) the Paris region and (b) the city of Paris 1975–82. Out-migration has provoked overall population loss in Paris itself and the three neighbouring, inner suburban *départements*. Within the city, eighteen of the twenty districts lost population. Population growth is now characteristic only of the outer suburbs. *Source of data:* INSEE (1982), *Evolution de la population sans doubles comptes par période intercensitaire 1968–75 et 1975–82: premières estimations* (Paris).

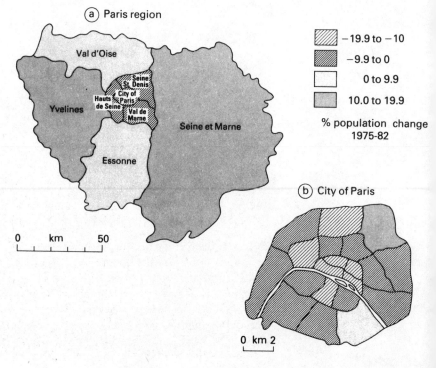

sharing in the slow-down in urban growth noted above for the USA and other parts of Europe. While it is very likely that the proportion living in towns and cities will continue to grow—perhaps to 85% by the year 2000—data for the period 1968–82 show a declining rate of in-migration to urban areas and the more urbanised the locality, the more marked the decline. Net out-migration rates are also declining for the rural areas and for many large villages net out-migration has given way to in-migration. Paris is no longer the point of convergence and is losing population, and there is considerable weakening in the attractiveness of most cities with more than 100,000 people. Fig. 4.6 shows that, for the period 1975–1982, all but two of the twenty districts of central Paris lost population (a total loss of some 131,000 people) as did the three immediately adjacent districts of Hauts de Seine, Seine St Denis, and Val de Marne. All areas continued to show a small excess of births over deaths, so the main contributory factor was out-migration. It is the outer suburbs that have continued to grow.

The developing world

The pace and extent of urban growth in the developing world during the present century has been quite different from the European experience. The urban explosion, especially over the last thirty years, has transformed the world pattern of urbanisation, producing a definitive shift away from the developed to the Third World. As Fig. 4.7 and Table 4.5 reveal, the old western European cities which dominated the scene in 1900 have now been replaced by cities of Latin America, India, China and Japan. The very size of city has become astonishing: by 1970 the smallest of the top 25 world cities was Leningrad with 4 million, a population as large as the second largest city (New York at 4.24 million) of 70 years before. Projections for the year 2000 also show changes of impressive proportions: there will be at least 25 cities with populations over 10 million, with cities like Mexico, São Paulo, Calcutta, Shanghai and Bombay coming in the top ten (Table 4.5) with 20 million inhabitants

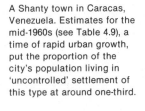

A Shanty town in Caracas, Venezuela. Estimates for the mid-1960s (see Table 4.9), a time of rapid urban growth, put the proportion of the city's population living in 'uncontrolled' settlement of this type at around one-third.

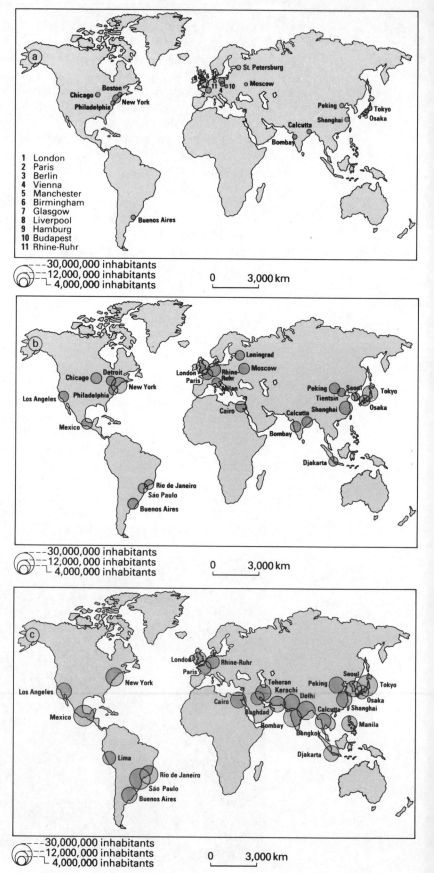

Fig 4.7 Population of major world cities in (a) 1900 and (b) 1970 and (c) projected to 2000. The growth of the third-world city is the most significant aspect of urban development in the second half of the twentieth century. The dominance of Europe and North America in 1900 gives way to the cities of Latin America, India, China and Japan. *Source:* Y. Charbit (1979), *La Population dans le monde,* La documentation française (Paris), p. III.4.

1 London
2 Paris
3 Berlin
4 Vienna
5 Manchester
6 Birmingham
7 Glasgow
8 Liverpool
9 Hamburg
10 Budapest
11 Rhine-Ruhr

30,000,000 inhabitants
12,000,000 inhabitants
4,000,000 inhabitants

0   3,000 km

30,000,000 inhabitants
12,000,000 inhabitants
4,000,000 inhabitants

0   3,000 km

30,000,000 inhabitants
12,000,000 inhabitants
4,000,000 inhabitants

0   3,000 km

Table 4.5 Population of top 10 world urban agglomerations in 1900, 1970 and estimate for 2000 (in millions). *Source:* as Fig. 4.7.

1900		1970		2000	
London	6.48	New York	16.3	Mexico City	31.6
New York	4.24	Tokyo–Yokohama	14.9	Tokyo–Yokohama	26.1
Paris	3.33	London	10.5	São Paulo	26.0
Berlin	2.42	Shanghai	10.0	New York	22.2
Chicago	1.72	Rhine–Ruhr	9.3	Calcutta	19.7
Vienna	1.66	Mexico City	8.6	Rio de Janeiro	19.4
Tokyo	1.50	Paris	8.4	Shanghai	19.2
St Petersburg	1.44	Los Angeles	8.4	Bombay	19.1
Philadelphia	1.42	Buenos Aires	8.3	Peking	19.1
Manchester	1.26	São Paulo	7.8	Seoul	18.7

Table 4.6 Population (millions) living in cities of 500,000 + , 1920–60. *Source:* Berry (1973), 76.

	1920	1960	% increase 1920–60
Europe	51.7	82.8	60
Other developed regions*	41.2	140.2	241
Third World	13.7	130.6	836
World total	106.6	353.6	231

*Includes Japan, N. America, USSR, Australia, New Zealand and temperate South America.

Table 4.7 Estimates of migration as a percentage of population increase in selected cities for varied periods between 1951 and 1968. *Source:* Berry (1973), 81.

City	Period	Total increase in population (000s)	Migrants as % of total increase
Bombay	1951–61	1,207	52
Caracas	1960–66	501	50
Djakarta	1961–68	1,528	59
Istanbul	1960–65	428	65
Lagos	1952–62	393	75
São Paulo	1960–67	2,543	68
Seoul	1955–65	1,697	63

each. The changing balance between developed and developing countries is shown in Table 4.6.

This spurt of urban growth represents economic and social change of revolutionary proportions. In many states where urban growth has been fastest, political and social structures are least able to cope and cities compete for resources in a national population which is itself doubling every thirty or forty years. The speed of growth, the lack of a proper industrial or economic base and problems in housing and social provision often mean that the result is apparent urban chaos. As elsewhere, growth is a product both of migration and natural increase. As Table 4.7 shows for a few cities in the 1950s and 1960s, migration accounted for between 50% and 75% of total population increase, and may be compared with the figures for West African countries in Table 4.8; or the data for cities in Bangladesh in Fig. 4.8. The preponderance of migration in urban growth is mainly associated with the early stages of urbanisation and yet the contribution of migration to urban growth is cumulative. Bryan Roberts has observed that though children of migrants born in towns are counted as part of the natural increase of urban places, even in those countries in which net migration contributes a minor fraction of urban population growth, the migration experience may still be an important one in the urban social structure. In Lima, Peru, the chances of a child who was born in the city having both parents also born there is less than one in ten.

Country	Period	Annual growth rate (%)		Migration as % of urban growth
		Total population	Urban population	
Gambia	1963–73	4.5	5.4	65
Ghana	1960–70	2.4	4.7	28
Ivory Coast	1965–75	5.2	8.2	59
Liberia	1962–74	3.4	6.6	60
Senegal	1960–70	2.7	4.9	40
Sierra Leone	1963–74	1.9	5.4	63
Togo	1960–70	3.0	5.4	44
Upper Volta	1965–75	1.7	3.4	55

Fig 4.8 In-migration as a percentage of population increase 1961-74 for Bangladeshi cities. Migration frequently contributes a large proportion of overall growth — 74% for Dacca, 73% for Khulna and 43% for Chittagong — as a result of migration from rural areas and small towns. There is, however, no general relationship between city-size and the role of in-migration in population growth. *Source:* A. Al-mamun Khan (1982) 'Rural–urban migration and urbanisation in Bangladesh', *Geographical Review* 72:385.

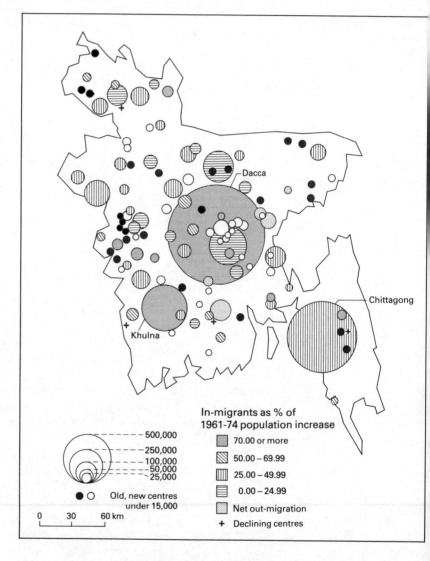

The countries of West Africa provide a further illustration of rural–urban migration. Complex migration systems have evolved within and between countries, with long traditions of temporary and semi-permanent labour migrations. The overall extent of urbanisation is still limited—around 30% in most states shown in Table 4.8, but the rate of growth has been substantial in recent years, exceeding in all eight cases shown in Table 4.8 the rate of growth in the total population. Migration

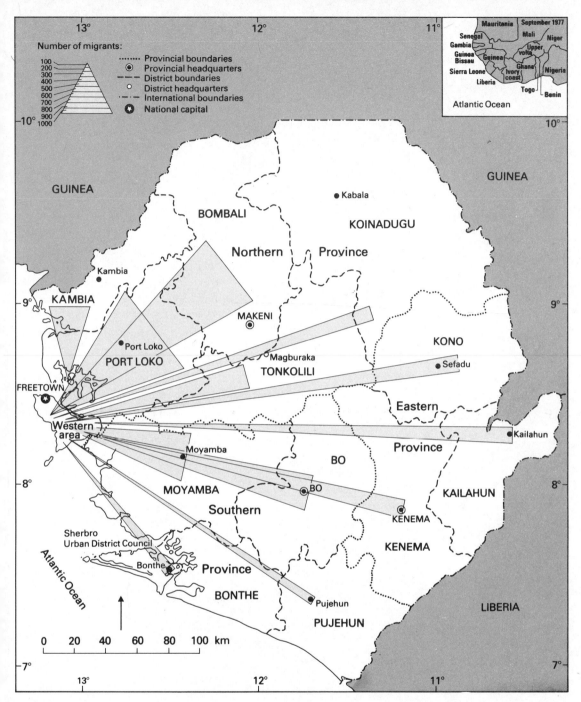

Fig 4.9 Migration streams to the Western Area from the Districts, Sierra Leone, 1975. Migration is a key element in urban growth throughout West Africa, contributing up to 65% of total increase. Freetown in Sierra Leone is a good example of a dominant capital city, recruiting migrants from all districts of the country. *Source:* Zachariah and Condé (1981), Map 20.

is a key factor, contributing on average a little under 50% of the total increase in city size. Between about 1965 and 1975, net rural−urban migration was 1.7 million: the migration contribution varies from 28% for Ghana to around 65% for the Gambia and Sierra Leone. The pattern of urban growth within these countries is remarkably tied to the fortunes of the largest, and often very dominant, city, a reflection of the colonial past. Thus in Ghana, the city of Accra had a net gain of 200,000 while smaller towns below 10,000 people experienced net migration losses. Dominant capital cities are also to be found in the Ivory Coast, Liberia, Senegal, Sierra Leone (Fig. 4.9) and the Gambia. Abidjan in the Ivory

Table 4.9 Extent of uncontrolled peripheral settlements in selected cities in the developing world. *Source:* Berry (1973), 84.

	Year	City Population (000s)	Total population of peripheral settlements (000s)	Uncontrolled settlement as % of city population
Calcutta	1961	6,700	2,220	33
Rio de Janeiro	1961	3,326	900	27
Mexico City	1966	3,287	1,500	46
Lima	1969	2,800	1,000	36
Caracas	1964	1,590	556	35
Santiago	1964	2,184	546	25
Maracaibo	1966	559	280	50

Coast had net migration gains from all twenty-seven districts in the country, as did Accra from all other regions in Ghana. Equally, although most countries have a secondary area of in-migration, it is very weak compared to migration to the principal city: Brong-Ahafo, the only other region in Ghana to experience net in-migration between 1960 and 1970, gained only 45,000 compared with a figure four times greater for Accra.

Obvious forms of maladjustment caused by rapid rural–urban migrations are the shanty towns on the edge of cities: the 'favellas' of Brazil, 'barriadas' of Peru, 'bustees' of India, or 'bidonvilles' of North Africa, squatter settlements of self-constructed huts. As the squatters generally have no legal right to land, they invade it quickly and *en masse*, suddenly confronting authorities with the established fact of their presence. The migrants in the developing world come perhaps less because of perceived opportunities offered by urban life than because of the imbalance between population and rural resources and they thus come, in their thousands, without job, home or neighbourhood. Providing themselves with a roof over their heads is a first priority; sanitation, electricity, and so on, come a poor second. The extent of 'uncontrolled' settlements means that they are everywhere in the developing world an important part of urban expansion: Table 4.9 shows that in some cities

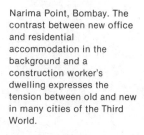

Narima Point, Bombay. The contrast between new office and residential accommodation in the background and a construction worker's dwelling expresses the tension between old and new in many cities of the Third World.

like Mexico City the proportion of population contained in them may reach almost half, while in many it is around one-third.

In many cities, therefore, a huge population lives in conditions of extreme social deprivation: in Calcutta, for example, the 'bustees' reveal images of social disarray, disease and poverty, difficult for the Western eye to comprehend. Many authors have described squatter settlements in terms of a 'spreading malady', 'fungus', 'festering sore' characterised by 'excessive squalor, filth and poverty... human depravity, deprivation, illiteracy, epidemics, and sickness...' Yet this is another example where applying Western norms and models of behaviour to other areas may lead to the wrong conclusions. For recent research in many countries has shown that contrary to some expectations migration on a grand scale does not always lead to material deprivation, personal and social disorganisation, political extremism or disruptive behaviour. Indeed, migration streams may be more socially varied than was once thought, strong cultural and institutional links between countryside and town may be maintained and, in any case, migration may tend to cream off the better, more motivated elements of rural society. African studies have shown that, while there is certainly poverty, unemployment, and crime associated with squatter settlement, for the great majority of migrants alienation, psychological stress and other symptoms of social disorganisation have been minimised by the ties of the extended family and those between city and village. Similar studies in Asia and Latin America have challenged what the American anthropologist Oscar Lewis referred to as the 'culture of poverty' where the individual has a strong feeling of helplessness, dependence and inferiority.

Others have thus argued that, far from being inevitably 'marginal' and 'parasitic', squatter settlements may play an important functional role as zones of transition within a society undergoing rapid urbanisation. Certainly some are 'slums of despair' but many represent a form of solution to the problem of housing shortage, allowing a dispossessed rural peasantry to adapt to a new way of life. Each city needs to be examined carefully and put in the context of prevailing cultural norms, the origins of the migrants, the formation and organisation of the squatter settlement itself. In some cases, levels of employment and education may be quite high, and one author commenting on Montego Bay spoke of the 'poor suburbanite of the developing world... upwardly mobile... industrious... a saver... more often a conservative than a radical'. Even in Calcutta's 'bustees' some researchers consider that they provide a vital mechanism for adaptation, providing accommodation, employment and elementary social organisation. These distinctions between the different types and functions of squatter settlements need to be borne in mind by policy-makers: many countries have regarded them as unwanted sores in the urban fabric and have tried expensively and with mixed results to remove them.

The countries of Latin America provide some eloquent examples of rapid urbanisation fuelled by migration. Rio de Janeiro, São Paulo, Buenos Aires, Lima and Mexico City have all grown very rapidly and are amongst the top world cities. Natural increase certainly contributes a great (and possibly increasing) amount to growth, but migration continues to provide the key to understanding the social geography of the city. The stereotyped view of the migrant as poor peasant pushed out of the countryside into an unwelcoming shanty-town on the edge of the city has been increasingly challenged. Recent studies have emphasised that often the migrant is relatively better educated, better informed and from a higher occupational background than many in his rural area of origin.

It is important to remember the variety of migrant experience. Many of the largest Latin American cities certainly draw their migrants directly from the countryside over very long distances, but the less important centres may draw in people from much narrower horizons and may themselves be but a stopping-point in a complex pattern of step-wise moves. It has been suggested that about one-quarter to one-third of migration to the large cities occurs in stages, while the rest is made up of direct moves and fill-in migration. The latter, documented in, for example, Argentina, Colombia and Chile, occurs when migrants move home to one location and then their children or younger siblings move on to new destinations. The process of settlement within the city has also been modified by recent research: studies in Lima, Mexico City, Bogotà, Montevideo and Santiago show that the shanty-town is not necessarily the first stop on arrival. Rather, migrants may go to rented accommodation in the city centre and then move on to the 'barriadas' subsequently. Many squatter settlements, therefore, are peopled by those born in the city or with several years' experience there as much as by recent migrants. Again, these marginal settlements may often represent an improvement compared with the central city slums and are themselves gradually improved over time. The settlements are generally well organised and, though they have great problems, they are not areas of deprivation, extreme poverty or disease. Some countries have tried to come to terms with squatter settlement by providing large-scale public housing schemes, as in Brazil, for example. Other countries have adopted a cheaper method and perhaps one more suited to the scale of the problem by constructing areas with services such as water, drainage and electricity but leaving house construction to the squatters.

Evidence on the characteristics of migrants comes from a number of countries. On educational levels, it has been shown for Lima that even in the 'barriadas' more than 90% of children attend school and that average educational attainment amongst migrants is higher than amongst non-migrants. In Guatemala City, of all migrants aged over seven years 31% have no formal schooling compared with 74% of the total provincial population. In social class, too, the average migrant comes from a higher class than is commonly supposed, the poor peasant being only one element in a variety of movements. As far as age and sex composition is concerned, again the pattern is fairly clear: migrants are young and there are more females than males. In Colombia, for example, 90% of rural migrants who left the countryside did so before they were thirty; while in Santiago for every 100 women migrants aged 15–24 there were only 64 men. This latter finding seems to be in contrast with other parts of the developing world where more men migrate than women.

A final strand of evidence of interest in Latin American studies relates to migration motives. As Table 4.10 shows, economic motives almost always emerge as the most significant, with social factors coming a poor second place. The search for a job is thus of primary concern, although of course other factors such as family links allow this motive to be satisfied and other elements such as the availability of health and education

Motive	Lima	Barranquilla	Monterrey	Santiago
Economic	61	62	70	59
Family/social	23	21	17	12
Study/education	9	3	7	10
Health	3	3	0	0
Others	6	11	6	19

Table 4.10 Motives for migration (percentages). *Source:* Gilbert (1974), 115.

facilities in urban areas may be the essential 'carrot' needed to transform a vague motive into an actual move.

For Latin America, then, as elsewhere, generalisations based on rather crude stereotypes of the migrant and his role do not stand up to the test of research. The migrant contributes to urban growth in all countries but migration streams are characterised by diversity. Migrants are as likely to be female as male, they may be married or single, they are likely to have established social contacts in the city before arrival and are likely to be quite well educated, to be young and to come from a higher class background. Recognition of these complexities is important for shaping policies and for predicting the urban future of the countries concerned.

Conclusions

The main thrust of this chapter has been to show the varied way in which migration has contributed to urban growth both for the nineteenth century and for the contemporary world. The accent has necessarily been on rural to urban movement since this has been a major motor of geographical change and the shift from a rural to an urban society is of fundamental importance for most states. As a footnote, though, we should re-emphasise that much of the movement currently associated with urban change is concerned with movement between and within cities, and even out of cities altogether. In the UK, the movement from the countryside has played itself out, to be replaced by migration between the major cities. In Latin America, too, much of interest for the future of cities lies in the way in which migration within cities will aid or hinder the process of social integration. It is to the fate of the migrant in the city that the next chapter turns.

5 Migrants in the city

Introduction

Most cities bear the indelible marks of waves of immigration. The broad
currents of movement sketched in Chapters 3 and 4 play themselves out in
the finest detail at the urban scale. We need look no further than Britain.
The population of New Commonwealth and Pakistani origin (that is, in
the main, from countries in the Caribbean, Africa and the Indian subcontinent) is strongly concentrated in urban areas. The 1981 census
suggests that some 40% live in Greater London, 20% in eight large cities
and most of the remaining 40% in smaller cities. Fig. 5.1 shows how the
size of the New Commonwealth population varies amongst urban areas in
England. It also shows that there is much variability *within* each area too.
This is particularly so in London: Fig. 5.2 maps the varying contribution
made by one group of migrants and their descendants to the populations
of different boroughs. In 1981, the proportion of the population living in
a household whose head was born in the New Commonwealth and
Pakistan varied from 33% in Brent to 2.4% in Havering in outer London,
and in inner London the highest concentrations were in the boroughs of
Haringey, Hackney, Newham and Lambeth. Indeed, if we look more
closely, we can see very definite concentrations within each borough too:
within Tower Hamlets, for example, Spitalfields ward records 57% of its
population in households whose head was born in New Commonwealth
countries. Other minority groups–from the Irish to the Chinese–also have
a marked tendency to concentrate in particular areas.

A family of West Indian
origin in London. The four
generations shown here span
the experience of migration
from the Caribbean to Britain
and the re-establishing of
family life.

Fig 5.1 Percentage of population in households with head born in New Commonwealth or Pakistan, English boroughs, 1981. The highest percentages are in London, the West Midlands and West Yorkshire. Note the considerable variations in concentration among boroughs and districts, especially in London (see Fig 5.2). *Note:* the width of each bar is proportional to the population in households with the head born in the new Commonwealth and Pakistan. *Source of data:* OPCS (1982) *Census 1981, County Reports* (HMSO, London).

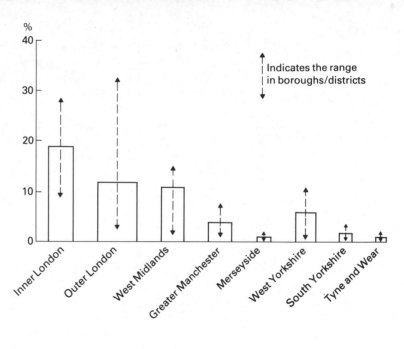

Indicates the range in boroughs/districts

Fig 5.2 Percentage of population in households with head born in New Commonwealth and Pakistan, Greater London 1981. Emphasises the considerable geographical variability of concentration. In Greater London as a whole, 14.3% of the population is in such households, a figure which spans 33% in Brent or 29.4% in Haringey and 2.4% in Havering or 3.8% in the City of London. *Source of data:* OPCS (1982), *Census 1981, County Report, Greater London* (CEN, 81 CR 17) and Table D (HMSO, London).

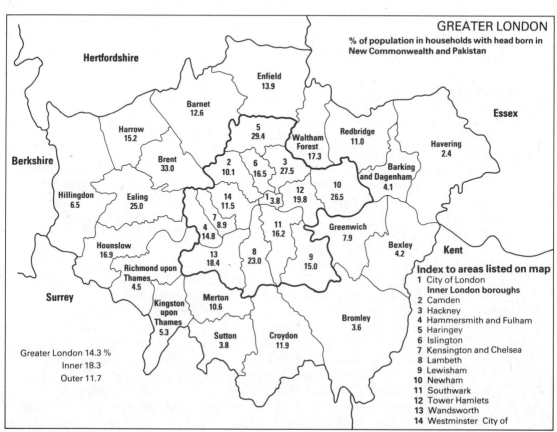

GREATER LONDON
% of population in households with head born in New Commonwealth and Pakistan

Hertfordshire

Enfield 13.9

Barnet 12.6

Essex

Harrow 15.2

5 29.4

Waltham Forest 17.3

Redbridge 11.0

Havering 2.4

Berkshire

Brent 33.0

2 10.1

6 16.5

3 27.5

Barking and Dagenham 4.1

Hillingdon 6.5

Ealing 25.0

14 11.5

1 3.8

12 19.8

10 26.5

Essex

7 8.9

Hounslow 16.9

4 14.8

11 16.2

Greenwich 7.9

Bexley 4.2

Kent

13 18.4

8 23.0

9 15.0

Richmond upon Thames 4.5

Surrey

Kingston upon Thames 5.3

Merton 10.6

Bromley 3.6

Sutton 3.8

Croydon 11.9

Greater London 14.3 %
Inner 18.3
Outer 11.7

Index to areas listed on map
1 City of London
Inner London boroughs
2 Camden
3 Hackney
4 Hammersmith and Fulham
5 Haringey
6 Islington
7 Kensington and Chelsea
8 Lambeth
9 Lewisham
10 Newham
11 Southwark
12 Tower Hamlets
13 Wandsworth
14 Westminster City of

73

The city acts not only as a magnet but as a melting-pot: people of widely differing culture, race and language may be absorbed into the population of the city. Yet, as London shows, this process of absorption is both halting and incomplete. Migrants frequently remain a distinctive element in the geography of the city, often in response to the extent of their cultural differences from the host population. It has been suggested that three factors influence the settlement patterns of minorities: the discriminatory attitude of the majority population; the community ties within the minority group and the degree to which they wish to be integrated with the host society; and the socio-economic status of the group members, often a very constricting factor. The study of social and geographical segregation has become a major focus of interest for geographers and other social scientists in recent years. There has been a considerable increase both in case studies of cities, especially in North America, Australia, New Zealand and Great Britain, and in the development of theories of urban social structure and of the historical evolution of residential patterns. There have also been recent pleas to see the migrant very much in the context of the economic and class structure of the city on the one hand and as an individual with a particular form of behaviour on the other.

While the major focus in the literature is on patterns of residence of ethnic or racial minorities, we should not forget the role of other migrants, from countryside to town for example, who may be different from the host population only because they are migrants. Nor should we confuse the existence of minorities in the city with migration in every case: a large proportion of negroes in American cities, Asians in British cities, or Chinese in the cities of Malaysia and Indonesia, for example, were born there. Nevertheless, to understand the city, it is certain that we need to grasp the forces that determine migration and settlement and how migrants contribute to the changing geography of the city.

Immigration and theories of urban social structure

In approaching the enormous complexity of spatial patterns in the city, the researcher has naturally turned to a number of simplified descriptions, or models, of social structure which summarise at least some of the variations within the cities of the developed world. Models developed in the 1960s and early 1970s emphasised the geographical dimensions of segregation and social structure, whilst more recent work has drawn attention to the structure of the wider economy as the essential background to how the city works. The role of immigrants has usually been pinpointed in the standard models.

Central to the ideas of the early urban theorists like Robert Park and Ernest Burgess, writing in the 1920s, was that of residential mobility. Park draws analogies from plant ecology, whereby competition exists between various population groups in the metropolis, the dominance of one group being replaced by the 'invasion' of another group through the process of 'succession'. The 'urban ecologists' thus suggested that cities were characterised by mobility of groups from place to place, upward social mobility involving geographical migration. The oldest-established groups move to new homes on the periphery as the city grows and the groups prosper, their place in the centre being taken by new arrivals. In his simple model of concentric zones Burgess recognised, though, the role

A still from *The Godfather*, starring Marlon Brando. The film was a powerful representation of the life and influence of one part of the Italian population in the USA, which maintained a strong family identity and links with native towns and villages in Italy.

of race and ethnicity in determining the residence of minority groups among the majority. Thus, he talked of the 'Black belt', of 'Chinatown', or of 'Little Sicily' in his description of Chicago.

Later thinking on 'social areas' in the city made more explicit the role of segregation and ethnic status. The original descriptive accounts by Shevky and Bell, and later elaborate computations based on varied data sets, isolate segregation as one of the three key dimensions in describing the differentiation of urban populations. The original findings for Los Angeles and San Francisco have proved applicable to cities in many parts of the world. The three dimensions recognised are, first, 'social rank and economic status' which tend to take the geographical form of sectors in the city; secondly, 'family status', where variables measuring family characteristics and the age of the population tend to vary by concentric zone; and thirdly 'segregation', where groups cluster in a particular part of the city. These variations are shown in their simplest form in Fig. 5.3. Of course, if we define more broadly the role of immigrants to the city, to include those from neighbouring rural areas, for example, then their role is wider than would be suggested by those models, for in many cities they are a vital element in the social mix in all parts of the city. Equally, many of the groups included under the third dimension of segregation may not be recent immigrants, but are segregated by reason of their racial or ethnic characteristics. Nevertheless, segregation is a feature of the most notable groups of migrants in the city, and understanding the processes involved is fundamental to an appreciation of how the city works.

The ways in which segregation occurs, the mechanisms by which it is perpetuated or destroyed and how it may be measured have thus given rise to much discussion. Two concepts are at the root of the migrants' role in the city: ghetto-formation and assimilation. Ghettoes, clusters of people of similar ethnic, racial or cultural background, may be a reflection partly of that group's rejection by the wider society and partly of the group's own desire to maintain a geographically based community. The ghetto may be either temporary or permanent. In the first case, the

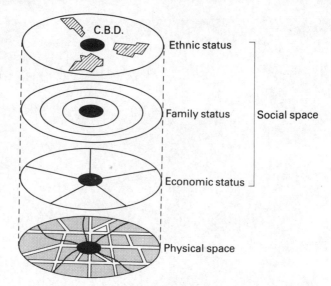

Fig 5.3 A model of the residential structure of the city. Super-imposed upon the physical space of the city, are various geographical patterns created by economic status (with a tendency towards a sectoral arrangement), family status (concentric arrangement of different family types) and ethnic status (clusters in particular districts). *Source:* H. Carter (1972), *The study of urban geography* (Edward Arnold, London), p. 278.

ghetto is a staging post between arrival of the immigrants and their assimilation into the city: immigrants find immediate refuge there with people of their own kind and then gradually, with a rise in socio-economic status and the acquisition of the language and customs of the host society, move on. By contrast, the permanent ghetto represents a barrier to assimilation since it acts as a means by which a cultural group can resist being weakened and absorbed into the wider community. It should not be assumed, though, that the ghetto is internally homogeneous. It has indeed been suggested that in large communities stratification develops along the lines of the host community, based on socio-economic and family status. Amongst the best-known examples of the ghetto are the Jewish enclaves in many cities of Europe and elsewhere before the present century. Equally, the mere fact of skin colour provides firm geographical barriers of residence between black and white in the North American city of today, for example in New York (Fig. 5.4). A further example, of forced ghetto formation, comes from South Africa where the policy of *apartheid* institutionalises spatial segregation. There is a marked concentration of blacks in small areas of Greater Johannesburg like Soweto.

The translation out of the ghetto takes place through the process of assimilation by which the various cultural differences gradually disappear. Minority groups may break with traditional life-styles and begin to feel a sense of belonging in the host society; they participate in the institutions of the larger community and form permanent relationships outside their group through intermarriage; they may take part in civic and political life and change their cultural patterns, including religion. Equally, assimilation may be accompanied by the decline of prejudice and discrimination by the majority against the minority. The rate of assimilation and its completeness vary enormously according to the group and the city concerned. Clearly language, religious differences, and above all colour, affecting international migrants, will prove a good deal more resistant to absorption than region of birth or occupation which may distinguish the internal mover from countryside to town. Yet even internal migrants may show considerable signs of clustering, especially in the early stages of urbanisation. Thus, Fig. 5.5 shows for Paris in 1911

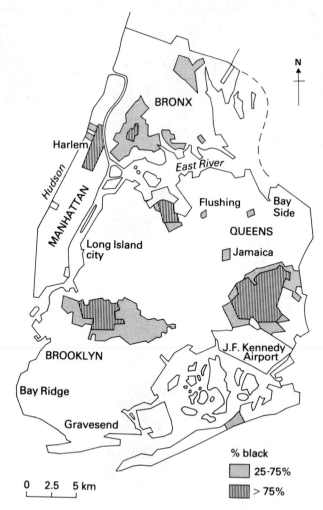

Fig 5.4 Black ghettoes in New York City. Colour has a major effect on patterns of segregation, such that in some areas of the city like Harlem or South Bronx over 75% of the population is black. *Source:* J. Broek and J. Webb (1978) *A geography of mankind*, 3rd ed. (McGraw Hill, New York).

BRONX

Harlem

Hudson

East River

MANHATTAN

Flushing

Bay Side

QUEENS

Long Island city

Jamaica

BROOKLYN

J.F. Kennedy Airport

Bay Ridge

Gravesend

N

% black

25-75%

> 75%

0   2.5   5 km

how groups from provincial districts of France clustered in particular parts of the city. This reflected the cultural differences of migrants from, say, Brittany or the Alps; economic contrasts within Paris in terms of industrial and commercial functions; and, perhaps most marked, the role that the railway station of arrival played in grouping migrants in that district of the city!

Much thought has been devoted to measuring the distribution and segregation of immigrants in the city. Simple maps of distribution obscure the importance of the size of population in a particular area. Location quotients are a simple answer to this, indicating the deviation of any population from what one would expect if the group were evenly distributed throughout the city. So a district in New York which has 2% of the city's total population and 2% of Puerto Rican immigrants will have a location quotient of 1. If the Puerto Rican figure were 5%, then the location quotient would be 2.5, indicating high concentration. It may also be used to compare the concentration of two groups. From Table 5.1 we see the way in which the West Indians in London were much more concentrated than the Irish. In 64.6% of districts, or wards, the location quotient for West Indians is over 2, indicating high concentration, whereas for the Irish the figure is only 26.9%.

A simple graphical means of comparing different groups, regardless of distribution in the city by detailed area, is given in Fig. 5.6, the Lorenz

Fig 5.5 Grouping of origins by *département* (a,c,e) and intra-city destinations by *arrondissement* (b,d,f) of migrants to Paris, 1911. There is a distinct pattern matching origins and destinations where migrants from the West (a) tend to gather in the western districts (b) of the city, from the North-East (c) in the northern districts (d), and so on. *Source:* based on P.E. Ogden and S.W.C. Winchester (1975) 'The residential segregation of provincial migrants in Paris in 1911', *Transactions of the Institute of British Geographers* 65:38.

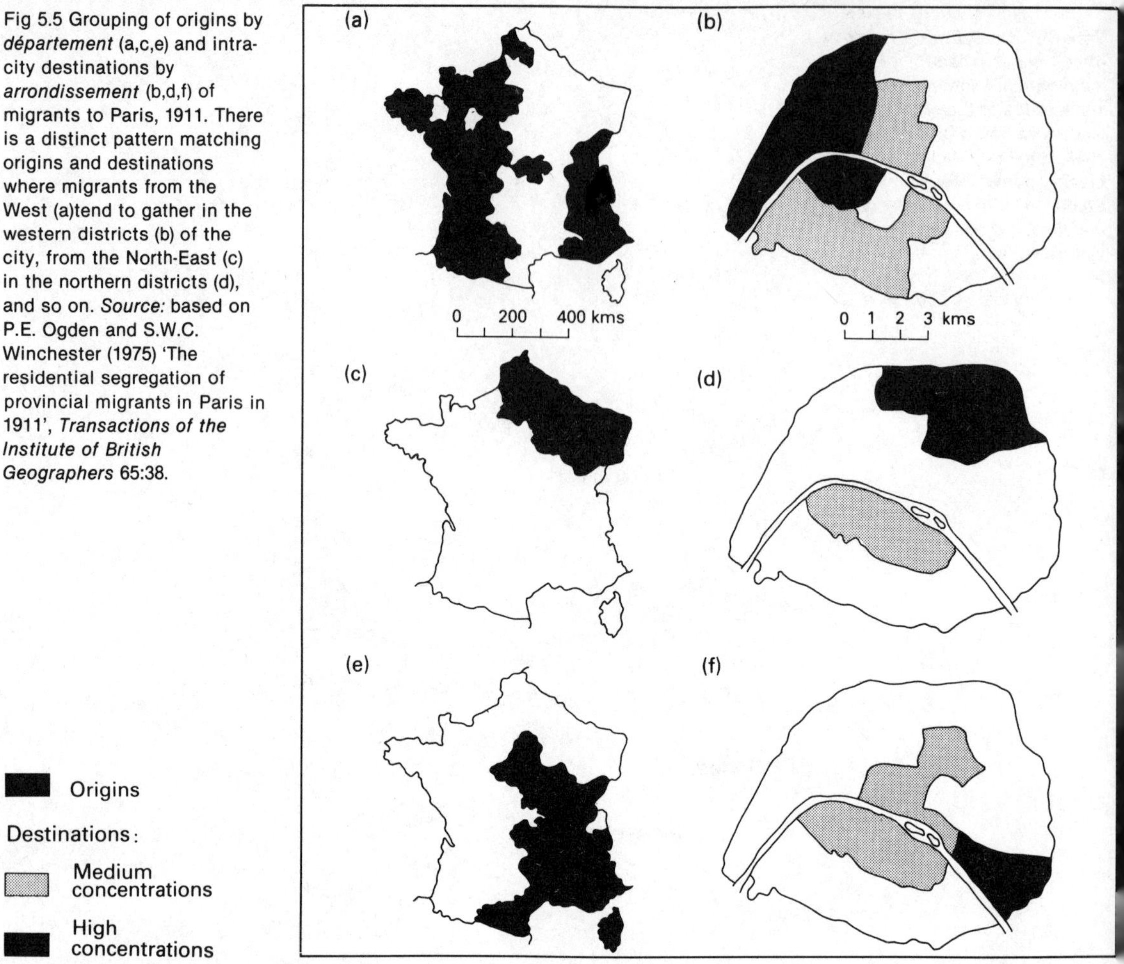

■ Origins

Destinations:

▨ Medium concentrations

■ High concentrations

Table 5.1 Percentage of wards in London with a given location quotient (1966 census). *Source:* Jones and Eyles (1977), 173.

Location quotient	West Indies (%)	Irish (%)
over 2	64.6	26.9
1–2	18.8	36.0
0.51–0.99	7.9	27.0
0–0.5	8.6	9.7

curve. This compares the cumulative percentage of each ethnic group in 611 districts in Melbourne with the cumulative percentage of the remainder. A straight diagonal line indicates no segregation, the UK group approximating most nearly to it; a strongly bowed line indicates strong segregation, as for the Italians, Greeks or Maltese in this example. This relationship may be given more precise statistical form through the calculation of indices of dissimilarity, very widely used in urban social geography of late to compare the distribution of two ethnic groups. The index is expressed in percentage terms, where 100 means complete segregation and 0 means no segregation. It may be calculated very simply from the following:

$$Id = \frac{1}{2} \sum_{i=1}^{k} |x_i - y_i|$$

Fig 5.6 Concentration curves
of the residential distribution
of ethnic groups in
Melbourne, 1961. Compares
the cumulative percentage of
each ethnic group in 611
districts in the city with the
cumulative percentage of the
remainder. A diagonal line
indicates no segregation.
Normally, the segregation
line is a curve whose
distance from the diagonal
(e.g. for Maltese or Greeks)
indicates the degree of
segregation. *Source:* F.
Lancaster Jones (1967)
'Ethnic concentration and
assimilation: an Australian
case study', *Social Forces*
45:412-23.

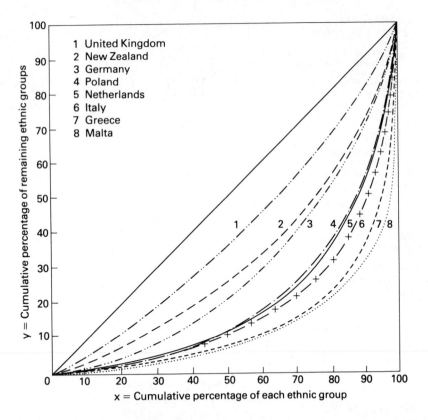

That is, the index of dissimilarity (*Id*) is equal to half the sum of the differences of the two groups, *x* and *y*, in each of the *i* units in the whole city or country, *k*. An example of data is given for the USA in 1970 in Table 5.2. The difference is calculated by subtracting the smaller of the *x* and *y* (black and white) figures from the larger in each of the regions (*i*) in the USA (*k*). The sum of the resulting differences is then halved to give the index of dissimilarity, which in this example would be 25. Thus, at the regional scale, 25% of the black population of the USA in 1970 would need to change its region of residence in order to replicate the regional distribution of the white population. Whereas the index of dissimilarity compares one group with another, the index of segregation compares one group with the whole and is ranged similarly on a scale of 0 to 100. Tables 5.3 and 5.4 give examples of the use of these indices for Chicago in 1950 and UK cities in 1971. In the first case, these simple calculations bring out not only differences between national groups, but also the extreme segregation of negroes compared with all other groups referred to here. In the second case, we see that considerable segregation exists in the British city, particularly amongst Asians, with figures for most groups exceeding 50%. There are certainly limitations in the use of indices of this kind, since they may be distorted by the size of administrative unit or the size of

Table 5.2 Black and white
populations, USA 1970.
Source: Peach (1975), 4.

Region	% of black population	% of white population	Difference
South	53	28	25
North East	19	25	6
North Central	20	29	9
West	8	18	10
Total	100	100	50

Table 5.3 Indices of dissimilarity for foreign-born groups and negroes, Chicago, 1950. *Source:* O. D. Duncan and S. Lieberson, 'Ethnic segregation and assimilation', in Peach (1975), 100.

Country of origin	1	2	3	4	5	6
1. England and Wales	—					
2. Irish Republic	28.5	—				
3. Sweden	29.7	40.2	—			
4. Poland	58.4	66.7	67.8	—		
5. Italy	45.7	52.0	60.9	52.6	—	
6. Negro	77.8	81.4	85.5	90.8	69.6	—

Table 5.4 Segregation indices in selected cities in UK, 1971. *Source:* (1) R. I. Woods (1976), 'Aspects of the scale problem in the calculation of segregation indices: London and Birmingham 1961 and 1971', *TESG* 69: 169–77; (2) S. W. C. Winchester (1974–5), 'Immigrant areas in Coventry in 1971', *New Community* 4:97–104; (3) Runnymede Trust (1980), 84.

Birthplace group	City of Birmingham[1]	Coventry[2]	Greater[3] London
West Indians	50	34	52
Pakistanis	} 57	70	55
Indians		59	39
African Commonwealth	54	52	—

population group, and they have to some extent mesmerised urban geographers, but they do provide simple descriptive tools as a background to understanding the processes which create and maintain or diminish segregation.

Movement in the city

The foregoing descriptive tools and models should not in any way be taken to imply stability in the geographical or social pattern of immigrant communities in the city. Intra-urban mobility has been an increasing focus for research, since it is the mechanism by which much social assimilation takes place. It is also a form of mobility which, as the Zelinsky hypothesis indicates, is on the increase. Intra-urban mobility is a major process underlying the evolution of the simple models of urban structure based on socio-economic structure, family status and minority groups. Geographical mobility may be an expression of social progress as the new migrant establishes himself or herself and moves up the social ladder. Whole communities may gradually disperse from their original area of concentration in the city. A classic example is the movement of Jews in London as shown in Fig. 5.7, from the original East End ghetto, into which poor Russian and East European Jews poured in the years before 1914; individuals and groups prospered and moved west and north. The most prosperous made their way to the West End and Golders Green, the less so towards Finsbury and Islington. Immigrants may react in very much the same way as those who have been resident in the city since birth, their mobility reflecting a desire for better housing, a better, more spacious, environment for raising children, or the need to match residence to new job opportunities. As with the population at large, much depends on the stage in the life cycle, age and family status. For example, whether the migrant is single or married with a family on arrival in the city very much affects his or her mobility. In Paris in 1975, for example, over 80% of Algerian migrants were male, and most were single, whereas amongst the Italians only 54% were male and many came with families. This affected not only their degree of segregation in the city (segregation index of 25% for the former, 14% for the latter) but also the districts in which they lived and the degree of their mobility in the city.

Some researchers have emphasised the constraints placed upon possible moves within the city. That is to say, that the real force may be not so much the desire to move as whether or not the individual is allowed to

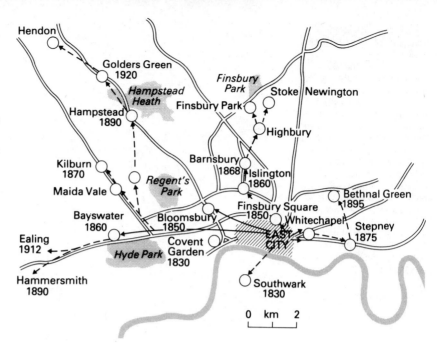

Fig 5.7 The spread of London's Jewish population from its point of origin east of the City. Immigrant communities may gradually disperse from their point of origin, in this case towards west and north London. *Source:* E. Jones and J. Eyles (1977), *An introduction to social geography* (Oxford University Press, Oxford), p. 184.

Hendon

Golders Green
1920

Hampstead Heath

Finsbury Park

Stoke Newington

Hampstead
1890

Finsbury Park

Highbury

Kilburn
1870

Barnsbury
1868

Islington
1860

Maida Vale

Regent's Park

Bayswater
1860

Bloomsbury
1850

Finsbury Square
1850

Whitechapel

Bethnal Green
1895

Stepney
1875

Ealing
1912

Covent Garden
1830

EAST CITY

Hyde Park

Hammersmith
1890

Southwark
1830

0 km 2

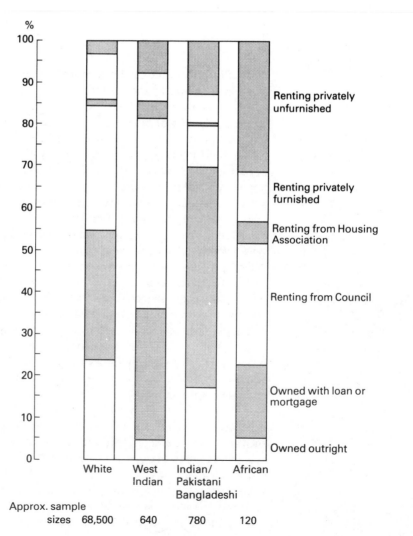

Fig 5.8 Housing tenure for head of household by ethnic group, 1978. Reveals contrast between the white and coloured populations and within the latter. The white population is much less likely to rent privately for example, and Asians are much more likely to be buying property than West Indians. *Source:* The Runnymede Trust and the Radical Statistics Race Group (1980), p. 77.

%

Renting privately unfurnished

Renting privately furnished

Renting from Housing Association

Renting from Council

Owned with loan or mortgage

Owned outright

White   West Indian   Indian/ Pakistani Bangladeshi   African

Approx. sample sizes   68,500   640   780   120

81

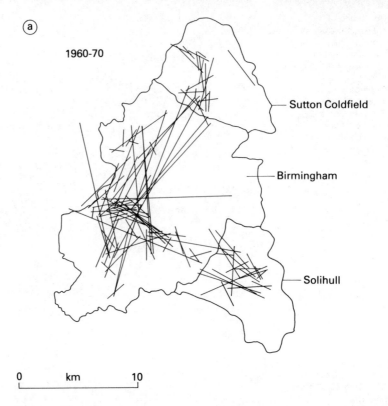

Fig 5.9 Migration of the 'Who's Who' élite 1960–70 (a) intra-urban moves in Birmingham, Sutton Coldfield and Solihull, (b) intra-regional moves in the West Midlands region, (c) moves between the West Midlands region and the remainder of England and Wales. Note the geographical bias evident in these moves, particularly at the regional and national scale, of businessmen, professionals, politicians and other worthies such as sportsmen. *Source:* R.I. Woods (1980), 'Migration and social segregation in Birmingham and the West Midlands region', in White and Woods (1980), pp. 191–3.

(a)

1960-70

Sutton Coldfield

Birmingham

Solihull

0   km   10

move. For few people can buy any house they wish in any area. Almost all are constrained by the need to obtain finance from building societies or others; or by the need to satisfy various conditions for public housing; or by the availability of other forms of rented accommodation. The relative positions of white and coloured groups in 1978 are given in Fig. 5.8, which shows the types of housing tenure for different sections of the population in Great Britain. There is a contrast both between the white population and the coloured and also amongst the latter groups. Many more Asians, for example, are borrowing money to buy their houses, and their use of council housing is only one-third of the national average. West Indians, in contrast, use council housing more than average and very few own their houses outright.

Geographical patterns of movement in the city show both directional bias and a 'distance-decay' effect. An example of the former has been provided by some interesting recent work by Woods on Birmingham which serves to remind us that it is not only racially or ethnically distinctive groups who have distinct patterns of movement. By using 'Who's Who' listings from the Birmingham Post and Mail Year Books, it is possible to show the migratory pattern of the 'élite' in the local community, including prominent businessmen, professionals, politicians and others such as sportsmen. Figs. 5.9a–c show the bias in the movement pattern, especially within the West Midlands Region (b) where migration is between the city and small towns and commuter villages in the south of the conurbation; and (c), where links with the rest of England are predominantly to the south and south-east. The movement of those in professional and managerial jobs, then, helps to reinforce their segregation in specific residential areas. As in so many studies, distance is a major constraint on moves within the city too. A recent study of Glasgow showed that almost 50% of moves made in 1974 were under 2 km, and

(b)

Destination

1960-70

0 km 50

(c)

Destination

1960-70

0 km 100

that the friction of distance varied according to tenure, reason for move, size of house and of household. For the extent of most people's knowledge about the city is restricted to the neighbourhoods immediately around them. Geographers' studies of people's mental maps, or images of the city have shown us how distorted they may be (see Chapter 2). An individual's information field is affected by such factors as shopping trips, journey to work, social and family visits and is, therefore, likely to be especially restricted in the case of strongly segregated migrant communities.

A summary of factors affecting immigrant settlement in the city: a New Zealand example

A recent study of immigrants in New Zealand cities has provided a summary of the various factors affecting their settlement, which reflect in part and expand some of the ideas presented in the first two sections of this chapter. Since the War, while migration from the UK has still accounted for a large proportion of arrivals, new groups have come from the Netherlands, Poland, Hungary, Western Samoa and the Cook Islands, while long-established groups like the Yugoslavs, Greeks and Italians have seen their numbers grow. There has been a strong concentration of immigrants in the Auckland and Wellington areas. As the variety of racial and ethnic minorities has increased, so the need to control immigration and to understand the processes governing segregation in the cities has been perceived.

The geographer A.D. Trlin in reviewing a wide body of literature from different disciplines has suggested four factors (see Fig. 5.10) which may be applied also to areas beyond New Zealand. These are:
(a) the process of migration
(b) population characteristics and urban ecology
(c) culture (ethnicity)
(d) perception and beliefs

The first very broad factor implies that the form and selective character of migration are determinants of residential patterns. So whether movement takes the form of chain or refugee migration, the nature of influences on migration at the point of origin and of destination and the

A poster advertising free lectures on New Zealand, with illustrations, on 14 November 1865. Information about distant places was gathered by a variety of means, of which the 'lectures to working men' in London were but one example.

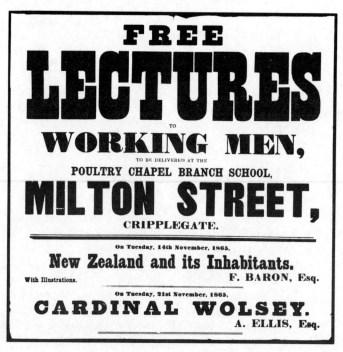

FREE

LECTURES

TO

WORKING MEN,

TO BE DELIVERED AT THE

POULTRY CHAPEL BRANCH SCHOOL,

MILTON STREET,

CRIPPLEGATE.

On Tuesday, 14th November, 1865,

New Zealand and its Inhabitants.

With Illustrations.   F. BARON, Esq.

On Tuesday, 21st November, 1865,

CARDINAL WOLSEY.

A. ELLIS, Esq.

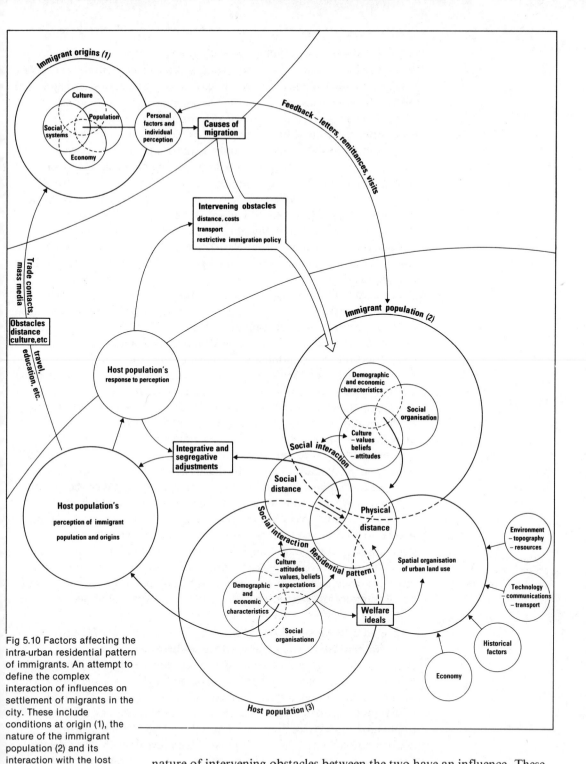

Immigrant origins *(1)*

Culture

Population

Social systems

Economy

Personal factors and individual perception

Causes of migration

Feedback – letters, remittances, visits

Intervening obstacles
distance, costs
transport
restrictive immigration policy

Trade contacts, mass media

Obstacles
distance
culture, etc

travel, education, etc.

Host population's
response to perception

Immigrant population *(2)*

Demographic and economic characteristics

Social organisation

Culture
– values
beliefs
– attitudes

Social interaction

Integrative and segregative adjustments

Social distance

Physical distance

Environment
– topography
– resources

Social interaction

Host population's

perception of immigrant

population and origins

Residential pattern

Culture
– attitudes
– values, beliefs
– expectations

Demographic and economic characteristics

Spatial organisation of urban land use

Technology
– communications
– transport

Social organisationn

Welfare ideals

Historical factors

Economy

Host population *(3)*

Fig 5.10 Factors affecting the intra-urban residential pattern of immigrants. An attempt to define the complex interaction of influences on settlement of migrants in the city. These include conditions at origin (1), the nature of the immigrant population (2) and its interaction with the lost population (3). These diverse relationships may be reduced to four main influences (see text). *Source:* A.D. Trlin (1976), 'Towards the integration of factors affecting immigrant intra-urban residential patterns', *New Zealand Geographer* 32,1:Fig. 1.

nature of intervening obstacles between the two have an influence. These are moderated by a variety of personal factors or perceptions. Potential migrants, for example, receive information about the area of destination via letters, the mass media, or temporary return home by relatives and friends which may influence their choice of destination both generally and specifically within the city. The major obstacles that may exist include distance, economic costs, availability of transport and restrictive immigration policies. The overall effect is to produce selective flows of migrants, selective ethnically, racially and by age, skill and general social and economic characteristics. An example is the Immigration Acts in New Zealand by which admission was allowed for most non-British migrants only if they were closely related to permanent residents in New Zealand. A classic example of the role of the process of migration is the establishment of the 'Little Italies' in New Zealand cities by chain migration: potential migrants in Italy learnt of opportunities, were provided with transport, accommodation and employment by relations already installed. This is very similar to evidence from the USA where links between certain villages in Italy and certain parts of the New York and other major cities are well known. A study of the years 1908–10 showed that 79% of all immigrants were joining relatives and 15% friends. Similar examples from New Zealand show how chain movements lead to closely-knit communities of Yugoslavs, Indians, Chinese, Cook Islanders and so on.

The second major factor—urban ecology—underlines the importance of the simple social structural models of the city. The spatial organisation of land use into industrial, commercial, residential and recreational uses, and the characteristics of the immigrant and host communities have a clear effect on the reception and settlement of migrants. In a newly growing society like New Zealand, the progress of urbanisation and what we may loosely term 'modernisation' is crucial. Studies of Auckland and Wellington have shown the validity of Burgess's 'zone in transition' and of the ideas of invasion and succession for at least some of the immigrant arrivals. The importance of the nature of the migrants themselves is reinforced by the recognition that by no means all migrants are poor and underprivileged: many come with education and skills, and different groups fit differently into the ecological models. Analyses of the Dutch population in Auckland, for example, have revealed that their social pattern in the city is very like the general model for the total population: that is, socio-economic status and family status emerge as key factors governing distribution, although there are factors like length of residence which are peculiar to them as an immigrant group. Samoans in the same city were much more dissimilar from the host population, with factors of racial composition, percentage of mixed blood, existence of decentralised employment centres and length of residence being significant.

The third factor of culture or ethnicity underlies much of the pattern of segregation in New Zealand as it does elsewhere. There are straightforward differences in residence between the older-established European groups and the relative newcomers. Race, language and religion are key factors aiding or restricting assimilation. These may be combined with a fourth set of factors—perceptions and beliefs among the host population towards immigrants—to produce a powerful set of constraints. A study of attitudes in Auckland revealed that New Zealand-born residents tended to divide immigrants into three categories: whites, non-English-speaking (continental Europeans); non-whites (Asians and Pacific Islanders); and whites, English-speaking (British and Americans). Table 5.5 indicates a classification of five groups on a range from 1, least favourable to 6, most favourable. There is a clear preference for European groups over the Pacific Islanders and this is indeed reflected in the actual level of segregation also shown in the table.

Immigrant group	Perception index 1970	Index of residential segregation 1966
Dutch	4.82	21.40
Yugoslavs	4.44	38.00
Hungarians	4.21	40.30
Samoans	3.61	40.31
Niueans	3.47	53.04

Table 5.5 Perceptions of migrants and residential dissimilarity: the case of Auckland, New Zealand. *Source:* A. D. Trlin (1976), 'Towards the integration of factors affecting immigrant intra-urban residential patterns', *New Zealand Geographer* 32, 1:74.

A further example of the straightforward influence of the host population's attitudes is illustrated by immigration policies. As in Australia, harsh measures have been introduced to stop Asian immigration, and at various times measures have been taken against most groups, like the Yugoslavs or Chinese, perceived as unlikely to assimilate easily. With respect to settlement within the city itself, steps have also been taken to encourage dispersal. In housing policy, for example, the idea was to disperse the Maoris, and the Pacific Islander immigrants, from the central city.

Conclusions

We have seen, then, that the migrant almost invariably makes a distinctive contribution to the geography of the city. The most marked patterns of segregation occur when the newcomer is clearly different, by race, colour, language, or religion from the host population, though more minor differences such as region of origin within a particular country or social area and occupational group can also have an effect. The examples given here have served to remind us how complex underlying causes of social differences within the city may be, and also to bring out the similarities of cause and effect from city to city. The factors brought out by Trlin's New Zealand examples have, therefore, much wider applicability. It is also important to remember that the social geography of the city is constantly changing. Individual migrants arriving in the city may change residence many times in response to their gradual assimilation into, or indeed alienation from, the mainstream of its life: migrant clusters form and disperse. Geographers thus seek not only to describe and measure patterns of segregation at a particular time in a city's history, but also to show how change takes place.

6 Migration policies

Introduction

Policy towards migration has in many countries, not least in the United Kingdom, provoked bitter and continuing debate. The perceived need to control, direct or at least influence migration flows is by no means recent, but it has been particularly during the twentieth century as the overall level of mobility has increased that political discussion has sharpened. This chapter looks at the types and aims of migration policy and by examining case studies looks in detail at the motivation and effects underlying policies in three contrasted countries. It is a natural extension of themes raised in earlier chapters, since specific policies have influenced migration patterns at international, internal and intra-city scales.

Types of migration policy

We may include migration policy within the rather nebulous term of 'population policy'. Yet efforts to control migration contrast quite distinctly with official attempts to regulate fertility and mortality, the latter being less easy to implement, though generally less controversial, and with less easily predictable results. It is much easier to legislate to stop immigration, once the political argument has been won, than it is to control, for example, the causes of death. Migration policy almost always reflects the complex interplay of prejudice, political expediency and occasionally a real desire for social improvement. It frequently reveals the contrast between the 'real' world and the world perceived by politicians and public opinion.

The Berlin Wall. A policeman in the Western sector of Berlin talks with his opposite number on the Communist side through a gap in the concrete blocks of the Berlin Wall. The Wall was built by the Communists, along the border dividing West from East Berlin in August 1961 to halt the flow of refugees to the West.

Although most attention, not least in the present chapter, is devoted to the controversy over 'foreign' migration of one sort or another, we should not forget that much attention has concentrated upon the regulation of other sorts of movement. Thus we may recognise two different sorts of migration policy. First is the regulation of international movements, most countries having gradually created increasingly impenetrable barriers to immigration and occasionally to emigration. Thus the United States and Australia have, during this century, refined their immigration laws in order to control both numbers and 'quality' of migrants. The countries of eastern Europe and the Soviet Union, by contrast, have devoted much attention both to keeping others out and to keeping their own peoples in. Secondly, individual governments have increasingly sought to regulate internal migration, for example to stimulate internal colonisation of empty areas or to influence movement from countryside to town. This is a less easy and less sharply defined matter, since there are no 'frontiers' to be crossed and the application of direct laws is for most states too heavy-handed. Rather, countries such as the UK, France or Italy have turned to the application of regional policies, or in the case of the UK to the concept of New Towns, one of whose aims and effects is to encourage migration in particular directions. A further aspect of 'internal' policy relates to the controlling of patterns of 'circulation' and moves within the city: for example, journey to work, where again the influence exerted tends to be more indirect, in the UK through regulating fare patterns on public transport or promoting job relocation through Civil Service decentralisation or the Location of Offices Bureau.

These types of policy underline the vital distinction between the rigid application of laws, especially at the national scale, and those policies that rely on persuasion. Occasionally, too, migration 'policy' reveals the grim aspects of repression and expulsion—for example the forced emigration of Jews from late nineteenth-century Russia or from Germany in the 1930s, or the expulsion of Asians from Uganda in the 1970s. Certainly migration policies in whatever form can have a powerful geographical effect—on the world cultural map, on regional growth or decline or on the social geography of the city.

Aims of international migration policy

The varied aims of migration policy may be illustrated by reference to international movements. Controlling numbers is usually at the root of such policies. In the United Kingdom, for example, the debate has always centred around the absolute numbers of immigrants who should be allowed in. As we shall see below, one of the most powerful political weapons of those like Enoch Powell, who stridently opposed immigration in the 1960s, was to produce estimates, sometimes fanciful, of the size of the immigrant, or coloured, community by, say, 1980 or 2000 if the then present trends continued. The culmination of such pressures is that current governmental policy in the UK, partly reflecting and partly fostering public opinion, is still much concerned with numbers of new immigrants, although these are now small compared with the size of the permanent immigrant community. Equally, in the United States in the early years of the century, much attention was devoted to controlling the numbers of new immigrants: increasingly restrictive laws limited inflows in particular nationalities. There are very few countries in the contemporary world which do not try to exercise stringent controls on foreign immigration. That is not to say, however, that the simple control of numbers is easy: illegal international migration continues to elude the control of some governments. Recent examples include the movement of Mexicans to the USA or North Africans to France in the 1960s. By their very nature illegal migrants are difficult to count: estimates for the early 1980s put the number of illegal aliens in the USA somewhere between 3.5 and 6 million, with up to 500,000 arriving each year.

Many countries, of course, have not stopped at limiting numbers. They have further sought to control the type or 'quality' of migrant. Migration, as we have seen, is invariably a selective process, but frequently the resulting flow does not suit the country of destination. Thus, increasingly sophisticated policies in the field of international migration select immigrants according to their race, nationality, professional or educational standard. Many governments impose health checks, while others favour single migrants rather than families or encourage migrants to take up temporary rather than permanent residence. The so-called 'White Australia' policy, for example, implies selection on racial grounds, but also on grounds of education or skills, the aim being to minimise problems of association and match immigration to the requirements of the labour force. In post-war western Europe, Germany is a prime example of attempts at selective regulation: in the years of rapid economic growth and high labour demand the Germans encouraged immigration of young, male, temporary workers from Greece, Turkey or Yugoslavia. In the late 1970s and early 1980s, economic recession and unemployment have meant strict control on entry and some voluntary repatriation schemes, although Germany is left nevertheless with a large, increasingly permanent and family-based immigrant community.

It is true to say that this second strand of policy is frequently designed by receiving countries with little thought either for the migrants

Refugees from Haiti housed in a temporary centre in Miami. Florida has become the point of arrival for a large, diverse and frequently illegal migrant inflow from the Caribbean basin. Stemming the flow of political refugees and others seeking employment has become an urgent issue in American immigration policy.

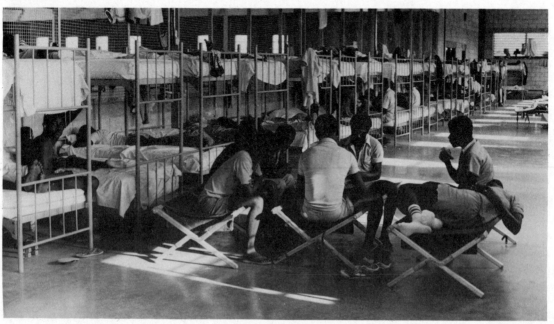

The arrival at Vienna railway station of Jewish immigrants from the USSR. Many make their way eventually to Israel or the United States. Obtaining permission to leave the Soviet Union can be a time-consuming and ultimately arbitrary process.

themselves or for the countries of origin, where the effects of removing the 'best' elements may be occasionally quite adverse.

A third general policy aim is of a rather different nature: to deal with the problems of immigrants once movement has taken place and the community is established. Policies of this sort have usually been designed to foster assimilation and minimise conflict between the new group and the host society. Thus, some countries have devised specific policies to cope with housing of immigrants, with the education of their children, with language training where necessary and with the limiting of racial discrimination. Others have encouraged naturalisation, while others still have tried to export perceived problems by encouraging repatriation. Within the EEC, the Netherlands is an excellent example of integrated policies designed to meet the needs of a new immigrant community, largely from former colonies in south-east Asia, which have met with a fair degree of success. In the UK, laws controlling numbers have, as we shall see below, been matched by, for example, the Race Relations Acts of 1965, 1968 and 1976. Policies of this type have been stimulated partly by the model of racial conflict apparent in the American city and partly by the realisation that many states which have imported labour have built up a permanent immigrant population which will remain regardless of laws restricting entry, and will probably grow through natural increase.

Aims of internal migration policy

Government involvement, by law or encouragement, may produce quite significant changes in the geographical distribution of population within states, too. Broadly speaking, policies of this type may be divided into two categories. First, governments have often played a direct role in encouraging frontier-ward migration and the expansion of otherwise sparsely populated areas. The development of the United States westward is a classic case, as too is the development of Siberia. In the USA, the early pioneer push west was matched by government annexation of land, railway construction and, occasionally, deliberate policy to aid in agricultural development. In the Prairies, for example, the Homestead Act of 1862 granted a free plot of 65 ha to every American who undertook to cultivate it and not to resell within five years. Since the Second World War, large-scale population movements of this type have been less frequent, and occasional ambitious government schemes have met with low rates of success: for example, the Russian Virgin Lands schemes or the transfer of people within Indonesia. It remains to be seen whether the recently united Vietnam will realise its aim of moving some 10 million people from the Red River delta to the mountain plateaux of the centre and the more sparsely populated Mekong delta area. The aim is to bring 5 million extra hectares of land into use by the year 2000.

Another example comes from Israel, where population redistribution policies have been in operation since the State of Israel was established in 1948. The aim was to stop the excessive concentration of the Jewish population on the narrow coastal plain and in a few large cities and to encourage the development of urban and rural settlement in the more sparsely populated peripheral regions of hill and desert country. One aspect of these policies was thus to contain the growth of Tel Aviv, Haifa and Jerusalem—which had over two-thirds of the Jewish population in 1948—and encourage the growth of medium and small towns, many of which were established after independence (Fig. 6.1).

A second type of policy is more specifically concerned with dealing with the effects of already established population concentration and regional imbalance. Many countries in the 'developed' world, for example, have devised intricate policies aimed at regional readjustments, in which migration plays a key role, either implicitly or explicitly. For urban and industrial growth from the nineteenth century onwards has increasingly polarised empty rural areas and densely populated cities. Thus, British regional policy since the War has had as one aim the reduction of the north–south drift; in France an intensive policy of regional diversification to counterbalance the growth of Paris has been developed; in Italy, a large-scale development scheme for the Mezzogiorno was initiated in the 1950s. Even in China there has been some attempt to discourage further settlement and indeed encourage emigration from Peking and Shanghai. Especially in the developing world, though, these policies often have limited effect in redistributing people, battling as they frequently are against the inexorable tide of concentration of industrial and commercial activities. Even in the Soviet Union centralised authority has only a limited success in controlling regional migration. In the developing world, as a 1978 United Nations Survey discovered, 113 out of 119 governments considered their population distribution unacceptable in some sense. Sixty-eight characterised it as highly unacceptable. Amongst the most frequently mentioned problems were disequilibrium in the labour market and excessive urban growth. Only 3 governments wished to increase migration from rural to urban areas, 23 stated that it would be desirable to keep migratory flows at their present level, 76 wished to slow them down, and 14 wished to bring about a reversal in migratory flows.

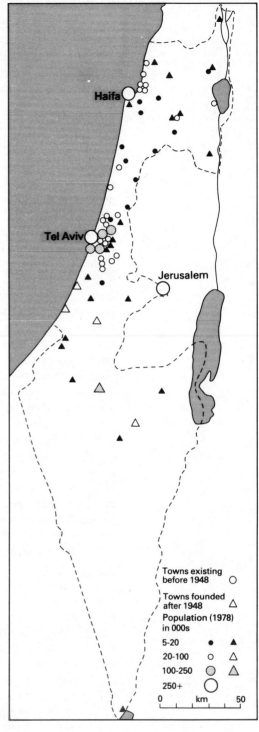

Fig 6.1 Urban settlement in Israel: towns existing before, and founded since, 1948. Population redistribution has figured high on the agenda of independent Israel. An example is the establishment of medium and small towns to deflect population growth from the main centres, a strategy influenced also by political considerations. *Source:* M. Romann (1981), 'Population redistribution policy in Israel: The special case of Jerusalem', in Webb *et al.*, p. 182.

Towns existing
before 1948   ○

Towns founded
after 1948   △

Population (1978)
in 000s

5-20	●	▲
20-100	○	△
100-250	◉	△
250+	◯	

0   km   50

Migration control in the UK

> *'We must be mad, literally mad, as a nation to be permitting the annual inflow of some 50,000 dependents, who are for the most part the material of the future growth of the immigrant-descended population. It is like watching a nation busily engaged in heaping up its own funeral pyre.'*
>
> (Enoch Powell, Birmingham, 20 April 1968)

The debate over immigration control has proved a stormy one in the case of the United Kingdom. The present highly restrictive controls are the product of a longish history of concern and gradual restriction, dating back well before even the 1905 Aliens Act, itself something of a benchmark. Indeed, T.W.E. Roche, in his book *The key in the lock: a history of immigration control in England from 1066 to the present day*, emphasises the historical antecedents of a phenomenon we frequently look upon as purely contemporary. The development of a comprehensive migration policy for the UK, still not complete, has seen a mixture of political expediency or necessity, much angry discussion, some prejudice, but with a gradual emergence of a consensus that a policy of some sort was necessary. Dominant themes have been the need to control numbers, especially from certain countries, the definition of 'nationality' and, latterly and haltingly, the need to accept a multiracial society, and devise policies to make it work. It has been with some pain, therefore, that the UK has moved from being a country of emigration in the nineteenth century to one of immigration in the twentieth.

For many years a *laissez-faire* attitude characterised British immigration policy, for example towards the large number of Irish arriving in the mid- to later nineteenth century. It was perhaps only with the influx of Jews after 1880—poor, speaking no English, concentrating in particular parts of Britain—that popular and parliamentary opinion began to call for restraint. This resulted in the 1905 Aliens Act, to be followed by the 1914 and 1919 Alien Restriction Acts, firmly establishing the principle of controlling numbers, the provision of the 1919 Act being renewed annually thereafter until the introduction of the 1971 Immigration Act. Recent immigration control cannot be understood, however, without reference to the 1948 British Nationality Act. The Act came in response to the independence of India and aimed to establish the rights of citizens of British colonies and Commonwealth countries to enter, work and settle in Britain. There were two categories of British citizenship—of the UK and Colonies and of the Commonwealth. Until 1947 the latter consisted of Australia, New Zealand and Canada, but during the 1950s and the 1960s former colonies gained independence and joined the Commonwealth, becoming known as the 'New Commonwealth'. Under the 1948 Act, then, the only persons subject to immigration control were 'aliens', that is citizens of countries which had no direct political ties with Britain.

It was in this context that the bulk of migration from the Indian subcontinent (India, Pakistan and the present Bangladesh) and the Caribbean took place. It was not that the Act encouraged migration; rather, it made legally possible a flow which other trends were creating. The demand for labour in Britain during the period of fairly sustained economic growth in the 1950s and 1960s complemented unemployment, poverty and population growth in these colonies and former colonies. Thus, between the census years of 1951 and 1961, the population of West Indian origin rose from 15,300 to 171,800; that of Indian origin from 30,800 to 81,400; that of Pakistani origin from 5,000 to 24,900; and that from the Far East from 12,000 to 29,600. Although the Conservative Government in 1955 rejected the idea of immigration control as a matter of principle, it was not long before the rising numbers of 'coloured' immigrants began to provoke political pressure for control. The last twenty years have, indeed, seen a gradual retreat from the 1948 Nationality Act with progressively more rigorous controls, especially on New Commonwealth immigrants. The Commonwealth Immigrants Act

Table 6.1 Estimated
population of New
Commonwealth and Pakistani
ethnic origins in Great
Britain. *Source:* Runnymede
Trust (1980), 7.

Mid-year	000s	% of GB population
1966	886	1.7
1967	973	1.8
1968	1,087	2.0
1969	1,190	2.2
1970	1,281	2.4
1971 (census year)	1,371	2.5
1972	1,453	2.7
1973	1,547	2.8
1974	1,615	3.0
1975	1,691	3.1
1976	1,771	3.3
1977	1,846	3.4
1978	1,920	3.5

of 1962 was introduced by the Conservative Government under pressure from MPs and some sections of public opinion, especially in the regions most affected by immigrant settlement: in 1958 black people had indeed been physically attacked in Nottingham and London and the 1959 General Election saw the reappearance of the former Fascist leader, Sir Oswald Mosley. The 1962 Act was subsequently strengthened by the Commonwealth Immigrants Act 1968, and both were replaced by the Immigration Act of 1971. For the experience of the 1960s had been both of continuing immigration at a high level and of escalating public and political debate. A leading anti-immigration figure was Enoch Powell, some of whose words are quoted above, who drew attention in a number of highly contentious speeches to the number of arrivals and the likely size of the immigrant population in the future, and raised the spectre of 'repatriation'. Race and immigration have been live issues at all the general elections since 1959, including that in May 1979 when Mrs Thatcher promised even tougher controls. Table 6.1 indicates the gradually growing size of the total immigrant population against which background this discussion took place, while Fig. 6.2 shows the effects on flows of newcomers of the Immigration Acts passed in the 1960s. It shows the peak of post-war black immigration in the early 1960s and also reveals the temporary increase in immigration immediately prior to the Acts. Thus, legislative control had the effect of increasing immigration for short periods.

The aim of the 1971 Act was further to limit entry, giving the right of entry to 'patrials', that is carefully defined groups of people who have strong, direct links or lines of descent with the UK. All aliens and all Commonwealth citizens who are not 'patrials' need permission to enter Britain. The administration of the Act is governed by the Immigration Rules which are laid before Parliament by the Home Secretary: these were altered in February 1980, amending previous Rules introduced in 1973. In addition, the Conservative Government brought forward a new Nationality Bill in January 1981, seeking to disentangle the complex web of entitlement to British nationality. The political preoccupation with controlling numbers has led to great concern over the immigration of families of dependents of those already settled in the UK and has led to some conflict of political and moral values.

Migration policy has, though, gone beyond the control of numbers and has sought to protect the needs of the coloured population. The Race

Fig 6.2 Population resident in Britain and born in the West Indies or India and Pakistan (and with one or both parents also born there, hence excluding most white people born there because of their parents' employment). Numbers are shown by date of entry into the UK and indicate the effects of the 1962 and 1968 Immigration Acts. Note also the temporary increase in inflows prior to the Acts. *Source:* The Runnymede Trust and the Radical Statistics Race Group (1980), p. 27.

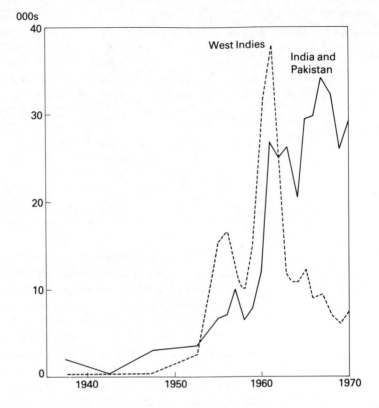

Relations Act of 1965 marked something of a watershed in British practice, making unlawful any discrimination on the grounds of race, colour, ethnic or national origin. This was followed by further Acts in 1968 and 1976, widening attempts to check discrimination. The Race Relations Board was set up by the first Act to investigate and deal with complaints. A further body, the Community Relations Commission, was set up in 1968 to promote harmonious race relations and to co-ordinate the work of local groups. The 1976 Act came partly in response to weaknesses in its predecessors and to research findings which showed that discrimination was still very widespread. A study in September 1974, for example, showed that 'an Asian or West Indian would, when applying for an unskilled job, face discrimination in at least a third, and perhaps as many as half of all cases'. This seemed to imply tens of thousands of cases annually, compared with the 150 employment complaints received by the Race Relations Board in 1973. So the 1976 Act replaced both the Community Relations Commission and the Race Relations Act with the Commission for Racial Equality, which was to have a wider policy role of enforcing the law and identifying and dealing with discriminatory practices at all levels. The role of such Acts lies, however, less in their detailed application than in the general, voluntary moulding of public attitudes. Riots in British cities in 1981—especially the inner-city areas of London and Liverpool—highlighted the need for much more wide-ranging government intervention. Poverty, poor housing and unemployment characterise many of those areas where the proportion of New Commonwealth residents is highest. Recent immigrants and their children have proved amongst the most vulnerable to economic recession, and the government has been forced to consider new policies—with a geographical dimension—to aid the inner cities.

Migration policy in Australia

Migration is at the root of Australian population and society, determining much of its population growth, cultural composition and geographical distribution. Australian attitudes to immigration and policy matters are in many respects in contrast to the British, but policy is nevertheless an excellent illustration of the interplay between the desire to increase or control numbers and to scrutinise the 'quality' or characteristics of immigrants. In the period 1788 to 1939, Australia received some 2.5 million immigrants, nearly half of whom arrived with government assistance. After the War population growth and immigration continued to go hand in hand. The population increased from 7.6 million in mid-1947 to 13.6 million by mid-1976, about 60% of this increase being due to post-war immigrants and their children (of which 41% was due to the immigrants and 19% to their Australian-born children). As a result, nearly 30% of the Australian population is either a post-war immigrant, or the child of one.

From the middle decades of the nineteenth century, the Australian government saw the need to encourage migration, especially permanent immigrants of British or north-west European origin. Indeed, there has always been a negative angle to policy: restricting the entry of the poor, criminal, lunatic or diseased and also of people considered difficult to assimilate or integrate. This 'White Australia Policy' was particularly designed to stop Australia being overwhelmed by Asian migrants of different cultures, histories and political traditions. Thus assistance with costs of passage was rarely given to Asians, eastern or southern Europeans: between 1788 and 1939 some 95% of assisted immigrants were of British origin. This racial and cultural discrimination against non-British settlers extended beyond the right of entry to cover civil rights, ownership of land, position in the public service and so on. By 1947, the result of migration policy was to produce an ethnic make-up of the population of 88% British, 7% north-western European, 1.7% southern European, 0.8% eastern European, 1.2% other whites and 1.3% non-white.

After the Second World War, attitudes began to change. Partly because of the wartime threat from Japan, Australians began to realise that their population was too small to defend itself and that a more intensive programme of recruitment and settlement should be adopted. In 1945, the government set itself the aim of increasing the population by 2% a year—half through natural increase of births over deaths, half through immigration. At first, the White Australia Policy was still the cornerstone of the government approach, trying to maintain the population of British origin. Gradually, though, it became obvious that Britain could not fulfil all Australia's needs and so successive post-war governments made migration arrangements with Germany, the Netherlands, Austria, Belgium and the Scandinavian countries as well as with some southern European countries like Greece, Italy and Spain. The effects of these changes are clearly brought out in Table 6.2. Nevertheless, discrimination against non-British and, still more, against non-Europeans was only very gradually reduced, many aspects being finally removed only under the Labour Government which came to power in 1972. For the first time, migration policy in Australia in the last decade, whilst still very restrictive, is not based on discrimination by race and on overwhelmingly favourable

Table 6.2 Birthplaces of foreign-born population in Australia, 1947 and 1977. *Source:* adapted from C. E. Price, 'Migration to and from Australia', in Smith (1981), 16–18.

Country	1947		1977	
	Number	% of total foreign-born	Number	% of total foreign-born
UK and Eire	541,267	72.7	1,123,272	40.4
New Zealand, Canada, S. Africa and other non-UK British	59,902	8.0	197,174	7.1
N. Europe	33,775	4.5	271,727	9.8
E. Europe	22,966	3.1	295,510	10.6
S. Europe	52,312	7.0	532,603	19.1
Others	33,965	4.6	363,800	13.0
Total foreign-born	744,187	100.0	2,784,086	100.0
Total population	7,579,358	—	13,814,908	—

treatment for the British. What has continued is a marked preference for educated and skilled immigrants, and direct government influence on the number of settlers. The provision of assisted passages, for example, has frequently been modified to suit changing economic circumstances. Concern in the early 1970s over economic recession, over the rapid growth of immigrant 'ghettoes' of Greeks and Italians in Australian cities, and over general notions of zero population growth and environmental control led the Liberal Government to reduce the 1970 settler target from 170,000 to 140,000. The new Labour Government further cut the target to 110,000 in 1973, 80,000 in 1974 and in 1975 announced that there would be no target at all and provision for only 20,000 assisted settlers. Nevertheless, in spite of the recession, net migration averaged some 40,000 per annum during the Labour Government's term and from 1976 the Liberal Government has pursued a cautious, although generally more encouraging policy.

Australia illustrates, therefore, a rather exceptional attitude to immigration. Within a general context of control over numbers and quality, it has encouraged movement as a basis for demographic and economic expansion. Above all, and in marked contrast to many western European countries seeking temporary labour migrants, its immigration policies have always encouraged the permanent settler and his or her family.

Migration control in the USSR and the socialist bloc

Attitudes to migration in the USSR and Eastern Europe generally are, of course, rather different from those in the non-Communist world. As far as international migration is concerned, rigorous policies exist in most states to control both emigration and immigration but the Eastern bloc serves as a particularly useful example of government influence on internal movements. A recent careful comparison of attitudes in the main capitalist and socialist states (Table 6.3) shows that whilst similarities are considerable, the socialist countries are more able to rely on measures such as residence permits, bans, and even exile for families and individuals or direct control over new construction of plants or removal of existing ones. Both employ a variety of incentives like the provision of industrial sites, job recruitment agencies, training programmes and investment in education, cultural facilities and housing, but Western nations rely more than their Eastern counterparts on indirect incentives to

Brasilia is a potent example of a government's ability to create new settlement patterns in which migration inevitably plays an important role. Here the 'dome' of the Senate is dwarfed by two giant towers of governmental offices.

Table 6.3 Comparison of major population redistribution measures employed in developed Western and socialist countries. *Source:* R. J. Fuchs and G. T. Demko (1979), 'Population distribution policies in developed Socialist and Western nations', *Population and Development Review* 5:449.

Directed toward	Policy emphasis	
	Incentive	**Disincentive**
Employing organisations	Both groups employ industrial infrastructure investments and transportation rate adjustments. Socialist countries emphasise job creation through direct investment in state industries and enterprises. Western nations rely primarily on indirect incentives such as grants, tax rebates, and other financial incentives to private organisations.	Socialist countries rely upon direct measures such as bans on new construction, or expansion of existing industries, and even shutting down or removal of plants. Western nations emphasise less direct disincentives: permits, licences, tax surcharges.
Individuals and families	Both groups employ social infrastructure investments (education, cultural facilities, housing) as primary incentives. Both groups use state employment or recruitment agencies to disseminate job information. Both groups employ job training programmes, and relocation grants. Socialist nations rely heavily on public housing provision and assignment. Socialist countries may employ mass exhortation and persuasion, and, in the case of the USSR, regional wage differentials.	In Western nations limited to tax disincentives, zoning and discriminatory hiring favouring residents. Socialist countries foster 'underurbanisation' and commuting. Socialist countries may employ administrative and legal measures, including residence permits, bans and exile.

firms such as grants, tax rebates and other financial inducements to private companies.

The dissatisfaction with existing population geographies and the need to tailor them more closely to the needs of centralised planning and state economic development is deep-rooted. The authors of the survey quoted in Table 6.3 have, indeed, traced back at least general guide-lines for a spatial population policy to the writings of Marx, Engels and Lenin. Marx and Engels in the *Communist Manifesto* (1848), for example, called for the 'gradual abolition of the distinction between town and country by a more equable distribution of population over the country'. Lenin called for 'the elimination... of the unnatural congestion of great masses of people in large cities' and for the 'unconstrained distribution of population throughout Russia'. Socialist states have not of course been wholly able to run counter to the general trend of urbanisation and concentration which accompanies economic development, but they have attempted to ensure a certain degree of regional equalisation of population, to avoid excessive concentrations in very large cities and to create a balanced settlement hierarchy. Much policy depends on the inherited geography of a particular state: the USSR, for example, has sought to control labour supply, especially labour shortages in Siberia and the Far North and surpluses in central Asia and the European South and Centre. It has devised various incentives and restraints, including regional differentials in wages, housing controls and social inducements whose effects considerably outweigh the more publicised and harsher measures of using criminals and others deemed 'undesirable' in unpopular occupations and locations. The latter method was particularly associated with Stalin—when some 12 to 14 million people may have been involved—but at present perhaps one or two million are still recruited in this way. A milder form of control of the individual involves police registration and work permits. Those with special skills, for example graduates of higher educational institutions, may be assigned to their first job in a particular location. Certain cities have restrictions on immigration which involve selection by skills or other attainments while the idea of 'under-urbanisation' has been widely used in socialist countries. Investments in housing and social infrastructure may be deliberately restricted, partly in order to divert capital to more directly productive economic sectors and partly to limit permanent migration to the cities. Labour needs may be met by drawing on surplus labour in rural villages and small towns: commuting takes the places of permanent migration.

Although socialist countries have potentially more powerful tools at their disposition for control over population flows, both they and the Western developed states have found that direct influence over regional growth and distribution is limited. Some 10 million people change residence annually in the USSR and the vast majority of these movements is unplanned, although one study estimated that in the western republic (the RSFSR) between 1966 and 1970 more than a million people were redistributed through government schemes. Over a long time-period, as Fig. 6.3 indicates, there has certainly been some redistribution of Russians eastwards from their traditional areas in the western USSR: the Russian population of the eastern USSR increased by roughly 25 million between 1897 and 1970, and whereas the western USSR contained 93% of the

Fig 6.3 USSR: regional
redistribution of Russians
into non-Russian areas of the
USSR from 1897 to 1970.
Compares the percentage of
all Russians living in each
region in 1970 with the
percentage in 1897.
Emphasises the general long-
term relocation of Russians
eastwards, although this has
been a halting process,
uneven in its effects. *Source:*
R.A Lewis and R.H. Rowland
(1977), 'East is east and west
is east ... population
redistribution in the USSR
and its impact on society',
*International Migration
Review* 11,1:10.

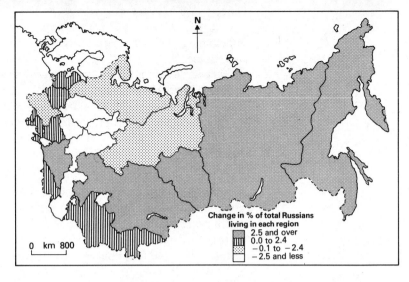

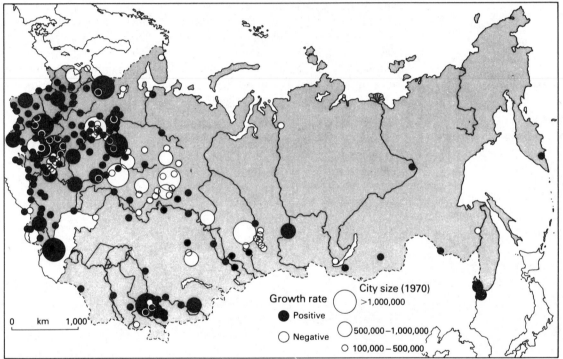

Fig 6.4 USSR: changes in
mean annual growth rates of
cities with populations
greater than 100,000 (1959-70
rate minus 1939-59 rate).
Almost all cities in the
European USSR west of the
Volga river experienced
increases in growth rates
whereas cities in the Urals,
western Siberia and parts of
Kazakhstan and the middle
Volga valley experienced
declining growth rates.
Source: P.E. Lydolph (1978),
'USSR: characteristics of the
present populations,' Ch. 6 in
Trewartha (ed.)(1978), p. 134.

Russians in 1897, it contained only 78% in 1970. Yet recently, this long-
term eastward trend has proved difficult to maintain and has, indeed,
gone into reverse: out-migration appears to have exceeded inmigration in
both eastern and western Siberia in every year since 1959. There is a
general, rather perverse, pattern of out-migration being greatest from
those areas where labour is most needed and for this amongst other
reasons Soviet planners have encouraged the location of capital-intensive
industries in Siberia and labour-intensive industries in the western
republics. Soviet writers maintain that policies have been successful, for
example, in keeping the sizes of large cities below what they might have
been if left unplanned, but judged against their own targets the policies do

seem to have failed. In addition, some policies have tended to create undesirable side-effects of ageing inner-city populations, labour shortage and an excessive reliance on commuting. It seems a sensible observation, then, that the patterns shown in Fig. 6.4—showing how different urban growth has been during 1959–70 compared with 1939–59—owe much less to government control than the government itself might have wished.

Conclusions

Migration policies are of interest because they represent concerted attempts by government to control the flow of people and to alter the geographical pattern of population distribution and characteristics. It is in their very nature to be controversial because they run against the 'natural', spontaneous movements that might otherwise take place. It is for this reason too that policies—particularly those seeking to alter regional patterns—meet with limited success, since they are seeking by relatively feeble government measures (even in socialist states) to reverse powerful economic trends. The most efficient policies are, perhaps, those seeking simply to regulate the flow of foreign migrants over national frontiers, although these too are rarely carried out without bitterness and resentment. A particularly striking feature, not least in the three examples briefly outlined here, is that policies rarely have as their main intention the improvement of the lot of migrants themselves.

Bibliography

There is a very large literature relating to migration, of which only a selection of the most easily available material is given here. Full references to material cited in the text are provided under each table or diagram as appropriate.

(a) General texts on population

Clarke, J. I. (1965, 2nd edn 1972) *Population geography* (Pergamon, Oxford).
Demko, G. J., Rose, H. M. and Schnell, G. A. (1970) *Population geography: a reader* (McGraw Hill, New York).
Harrison, G. A. and Boyce, A. J. (1972) *The structure of human populations* (Clarendon Press, Oxford).
Hornby, W. T. and Jones, M. (1980) *An introduction to population geography* (Cambridge University Press, Cambridge).
Jones, H. (1981) *A population geography* (Harper and Row, London).
Petersen, W. (1975) *Population* (Collier Macmillan, London) 3rd edn.
Sauvy, A. (1969) *General theory of population* (Weidenfeld and Nicolson, London)
Scientific American (1974) *The human population* (Scientific American, San Francisco).
Woods, R. I. (1979) *Population analysis in geography* (Longman, London).
   (1982) *Theoretical population geography* (Longman, London).
Young, L. B. (ed.) (1968) *Population in perspective* (Oxford University Press, Oxford).
Zelinsky, W. (1970) *A prologue to population geography* (Prentice Hall, London).
Zelinsky, W., Kosiński, L. A. and Prothero, R. M. (eds.) (1970) *Geography and a crowding world* (Oxford University Press, Oxford).

(b) General texts on migration

Brown, A. A. and Neuberger, E. (1977) *Internal migration: a comparative perspective* (Academic Press, London).
Courgeau, D. (1980) *Analyse quantitative des migrations humaines* (Masson, Paris).
Jackson, J. A. (ed.) (1969) *Migration* (Cambridge University Press, Cambridge).
Kosiński, L. A. and Prothero, R. M. (eds.) (1975) *People on the move* (Methuen, London).
Kritz, M. M., Keely, C. B. and Tomasi, S. (1981) *Global trends in migration* (Center for Migration Studies, New York).
Kubat, D. (1979) *The politics of migration policies* (Center for Migration Studies, New York).
Lewis, G. J. (1982) *Migration* (Croom Helm, London).
McNeill, W. H. and Adams, R. S. (eds.) (1978) *Human migration, patterns and policies* (Indiana University Press, Bloomington).
Open University (1974) *The micro-approach: economic and social surfaces. Unit 9, Human migration; Unit 10, The consequences of labour migration* (Open University Press, Milton Keynes).
Richmond, A. H. and Kubat, D. (1976) *Internal migration: the new world and the third world* (Sage, London).
Shaw, R. P. (1975) *Migration theory and fact* (Regional Science Research Institute, Philadelphia).
White, P. E. and Woods, R. I. (eds.) (1980) *The geographical impact of migration* (Longman, London).
Willis, K. (1974) *Problems in migration analysis* (Saxon House, Farnborough).

(c) Further reading

Included here are further items which are of particular value in following up the themes of the text. One source is articles in periodicals and journals. Most geographical and demographic journals contain occasional articles on migration. Up-to-date information on the UK may be found in *Population Trends* or *New Community*; a variety of interesting articles in *International Migration Review* and in *Migration Today*; and the new journal *Immigrants and Minorities* deals particularly with the historical dimensions of current patterns.

The *Geographical Magazine* contains articles of use to the 'A' level student. On migration see the series 'Immigrants and the City', edited by P. E. Ogden and P. Jackson, which ran from May to October 1982 in Vol. 54. The articles included were:

Eyles, J., 'Black and British' (May, No. 5), 277–83.

Ogden, P. E., 'France adapts to immigration with difficulty' (June, No. 6), 318–23.

Ward, D. 'The North American ghetto' (July, No. 7), 378–80.

Jackson, P., 'New York's minorities remain individual' (August, No. 8), 452–7.

Gould, W. T., 'Emigrants from fear' (September, No. 9), 494–8.

Burnley, I. H. 'Where the British are immigrants' (October, No. 10), 560–3.

Other recent relevant articles in the *Geographical Magazine* include:

Freeberne, M. (1981) 'Chinese succeed in the UK: immigrants retain identity', **53**, No. 11, 706–11.

Goddard, J. B. (1981) 'British cities in transition', **53**, No. 8, 523–30.

King, R. (1980) 'Cypriot refugees in Cyprus', **52**, No. 4, 266–73.

Learmonth, A. T. (1981) 'East Enders see Bangladesh: background to Bengali immigration', **53**, No. 7, 425–30.

Pooley, C. G. (1980) 'Local and national sources', **53**, No. 3, 205–8.

An article referred to in Chapter 2 is:

Wolpert, J. (1965) 'Behavioural aspects of the decision to migrate', *Papers and Proceedings, Regional Science Association* **15**, 159–69.

Other books which allow themes in the text to be explored in more detail are listed below. In the interests of brevity, articles in periodicals are not included.

Amin, S. (ed.) (1974) *Modern migrations in West Africa* (Oxford University Press, Oxford).

Barker, T. and Drake, M. (eds.) (1982) *Population and society in Britain 1850–1980* (Batsford, London).

Bechhofer, F. (ed.) (1969) *Population growth and the brain drain* (Edinburgh University Press, Edinburgh).

Bean, F. D. and Frisbie, W. P. (eds.) (1978) *The demography of racial and ethnic groups* (Academic Press, London).

Berger, J. and Mohr, J. (1975) *A seventh man: a book of images and words about the experience of migrant workers in Europe* (Penguin, Harmondsworth).

Berry, B. J. L. (1973) *The human consequences of urbanisation* (Macmillan, London). (1976) *Urbanisation and counterurbanisation* (Sage, London).

Birks, J. S. and Sinclair, C. A. (1980) *International migration and development in the Arab region* (ILO, Geneva).

Bodnar, J. E. (ed.) (1973) *The ethnic experience in Pennsylvania* (Bucknell University Press, Lewisburg).

Böhning, W. R. (1972) *The migration of workers in the United Kingdom and the European Community* (Oxford University Press, Oxford).

Braham, P., Rhodes, E. and Pearn, M. (eds.) (1981) *Discrimination and disadvantage in employment: the experience of black workers* (Harper and Row, London).

Brown, D. L. and Wardwell, J. M. (eds.) (1980) *New directions in urban–rural migration, the population turnaround in rural America* (Academic Press, London).

Castles, S and Kosack, G. (1973) *Immigrant workers and class structure in Western Europe* (Oxford University Press, Oxford).

Clark, W. A. V. and Moore, E. G. (1980) *Residential mobility and public policy* (Sage, London).

Clarke, J. I. and Kosiński, L. A. (1982) *Redistribution of Population in Africa* (Heinemann, London).

Coleman, D. A. (ed.) (1982) *Demography of immigrants and minority groups in the UK* (Academic Press, London).

Cornelius, W. A. (1978) *Mexican migration to the United States: causes, consequences and US responses* (Center for International Studies, MIT, Cambridge, Mass.).

Corwin, A. F. (ed.) (1978) *Immigrants–and immigrants: perspectives on Mexican labour migration to the United States* (Greenwood Press, Westport, Conn.).

Courgeau, D. (1970) *Les champs migratoires en France,* Cahier de l'I.N.E.D. 58 (Presses Universitaires de France, Paris).

Deakin, N. and Ungerson, C. (1977) *Leaving London: planned mobility and the inner city* (Heinemann, London).

Dench, G. (1975) *Maltese in London, a case-study in the erosion of ethnic consciousness* (Routledge and Kegan Paul, London).

Dinnerstein, L. and Reimers, D. M. (1977) *Ethnic Americans: a history of immigration and assimilation* (New York University Press, New York).

Dwyer, D. J. (1975) *People and housing in Third World cities, perspectives on the problem of spontaneous settlements* (Longman, London).

Dyer, C. (1978) *Population and society in twentieth-century France* (Hodder and Stoughton, London).

Easterlin, R. A. (ed.) (1980) *Population and economic change in developing countries* (Chicago University Press, Chicago).

Erickson, C. (1972) *Invisible immigrants: the adaptation of English and Scottish immigrants in nineteenth-century America* (Leicester University Press, Leicester).

(1976) *Emigration from Europe 1815–1914* (Black, London).

Fielding, A. J. (1982) *Counterurbanisation in Western Europe, Progress in Planning* 17, Pt 1 (Pergamon, Oxford).

Freeman, G. P. (1979) *Immigrant labour and racial conflict in industrial societies* (Princeton University Press, Princeton, NJ).

Garrard, J. A. (1971) *The English and immigration: a comparative study of the Jewish influx 1880–1910* (Oxford University Press, Oxford).

Gilbert, A. (1974) *Latin American development: a geographical perspective* (Penguin, Harmondsworth).

(ed.) (1976) *Development planning and spatial structure* (Wiley, London).

Gilbert, A. and Gugler, J. (1982) *Cities, poverty and development, urbanisation in the Third World* (Oxford University Press, Oxford).

Gould, P. and White, R. (1974) *Mental maps* (Penguin, Harmondsworth).

Gravier, J.-F. (1947) *Paris et le désert français* (Le Portulan, Paris).

Hakim, C. (1982) *Secondary analysis in social research, a guide to data sources and methods with examples* (George Allen and Unwin, London).

Hall, P. and Hay, D. (1980) *Growth centres in the European urban system* Heinemann, London).

Hall, R. and Ogden, P. E. (1983) *Europe's population in the 1970s and 1980s* (Department of Geography, Queen Mary College, London: Special Publication 4).

Handlin, O. (1941, new edn 1969) *Boston's immigrants: a study in acculturation* (Belknap Press of Harvard University Press, Cambridge, Mass.).

(1959) *Immigration as a factor in American history* (Prentice Hall, Englewood Cliffs, NJ).

Hill, D. (1972) *Great emigrations: I The Scots to Canada* (Gentry, London).

Hobcraft, J. and Rees, P. (1977) *Regional demographic development* (Croom Helm, London).

Holmes, C. (1978) *Immigrants and minorities in British society* (George Allen and Unwin, London).

Howe, I. (1976) *The immigrant Jews of New York 1881 to the present* (Routledge and Kegan Paul, London).

Hvidt, K. (1975) *Flight to America: the social background of 300,000 Dutch emigrants* (Academic Press, London).

Johnson, D. M. and Campbell, R. R. (1981) *Black migration in America, a social demographic history* (Duke University Press, Durham, NC).

Johnson, J. H., Salt, J. and Wood, P. A. (1974) *Housing and migration of labour in England and Wales* (Saxon House, Farnborough).

Jones, C. (1977) *Immigration and social policy in Britain* (Tavistock, London).

Jones, E. and Eyles, J. (1977) *An introduction to social geography* (Oxford University Press, Oxford).

Krausz, E. (1972) *Ethnic minorities in Britain* (Paladin, London).

Lawton, R. (1978) 'Population and society 1730–1900', in R. A. Dodgshon and R. A. Butlin (eds.), *An historical geography of England and Wales* (Academic Press, London).

Lee, T. R. (1977) *Race and residence: concentration and dispersal of immigrants in London* (Oxford University Press, Oxford).

Lloyd, P. (1979) *Slums of hope? Shanty towns of the Third World* (Penguin, Harmondsworth).

Merlin, P. (1971) *L'exode rural*, Cahier de l'I.N.E.D. 59, (Presses Universitaires de France, Paris).

Michel, A. (1974) *The modernisation of North African families in the Paris area* (Mouton, The Hague).

Miles, R. (1982) *Racism and migrant labour* (Routledge and Kegan Paul, London).

Milward, A. and Saul, S. B. (1973) *The economic development of continental Europe 1780–1870* (George Allen and Unwin, London).

Peach, C. (1968) *West Indian migration to Britain* (Oxford University Press, Oxford).

(1975) *Urban social segregation* (Longman, London).

Peach, C., Robinson, V. and Smith, S. (eds.) (1981) *Ethnic segregation in cities* (Croom Helm, London).

Piore, M. J. (1979) *Birds of passage: migrant labour and industrial societies* (Cambridge University Press, Cambridge).

Power, J. (1979) *Migrant workers in Western Europe and the United States* (Pergamon, Oxford).

Price, C. A. (1963) *Southern Europeans in Australia* (Oxford University Press, Oxford).

(ed.) (1975) *Greeks in Australia* (Australian National University Press, Canberra).

Redford, A. (1926, 3rd edn 1976) *Labour migration in England 1800–1850* (Manchester University Press, Manchester).

Rex, J. and Moore, R. (1967) *Race, community and conflict, a study of Sparkbrook* (Oxford University Press, Oxford, for Institute of Race Relations).

Roberts, B. (1978) *Cities of peasants* (Arnold, London).

Roche, T. W. E. (1969) *The key in the lock: immigration control in England from 1066 to the present day* (John Murray, London).

Rowland, D. T. (1979) *Internal migration in Australia* (Australian Bureau of Statistics, Canberra).

Runblom, H. and Norman, H. (eds.) (1976) *From Sweden to America: a history of the migration* (University of Minnesota Press, Minneapolis).

Runnymede Trust and the Radical Statistics Race Group (1980) *Britain's black population* (Heinemann, London).

Salt, J. and Clout, H. (eds.) (1976) *Migration in post-war Europe* (Oxford University Press, Oxford).

Scott, F. D. (ed.) (1968) *World migration in modern times* (Prentice Hall, New York).

Shevky, E. and Bell, W. (1955) *Social area analysis: theory, illustrative application and computational procedures* (Stanford University Press, Stanford).

Smith, T. E. (1981) *Commonwealth migration, flows and policies* (Macmillan, London).

Sundquist, J. L. (1975) *Dispersing population: what America can learn from Europe* (Brookings Institution, Washington, DC).

Tapinos, G. (1975) *L'immigration étrangère en France,* Cahier de l'I.N.E.D. 71 (Presses Universitaires de France, Paris).

Thomas, B. (1954, 2nd edn, 1973) *Migration and economic growth* (Cambridge University Press, Cambridge).

(1972) *Migration and urban development* (Methuen, London).

Todaro, M. P. (1976) *Internal migration in developing countries* (ILO, Geneva).

Trewartha, G. (ed.) (1978) *The more developed realm: a geography of its population* (Pergamon, Oxford).

Van Amersfoort, H. (1982) *Immigration and the formation of minority groups: the Dutch experience 1945–1975* (Cambridge University Press, Cambridge; Dutch edn 1974).

Ward, D. (1971) *Cities and immigrants* (Oxford University Press, Oxford).

Webb, J. W., Naukkarinen, A. and Kosiński, L. A. (1981) *Policies of population redistribution* (Geographical Society of Northern Finland for the IGU Commission on Population Geography, Oulu, Finland).

Weber, E. (1976) *Peasants into Frenchmen: the modernisation of rural France 1870–1914* (Stanford University Press, Stanford).

Willigan, J. D. and Lynch, K. A. (1982) *Sources and methods of historical demography* (Academic Press, London).

Zachariah, K. C. and Condé, J. (1981) *Migration in West Africa, demographic aspects* (Oxford University Press, Oxford).

Index